The Letters of John Wordsworth

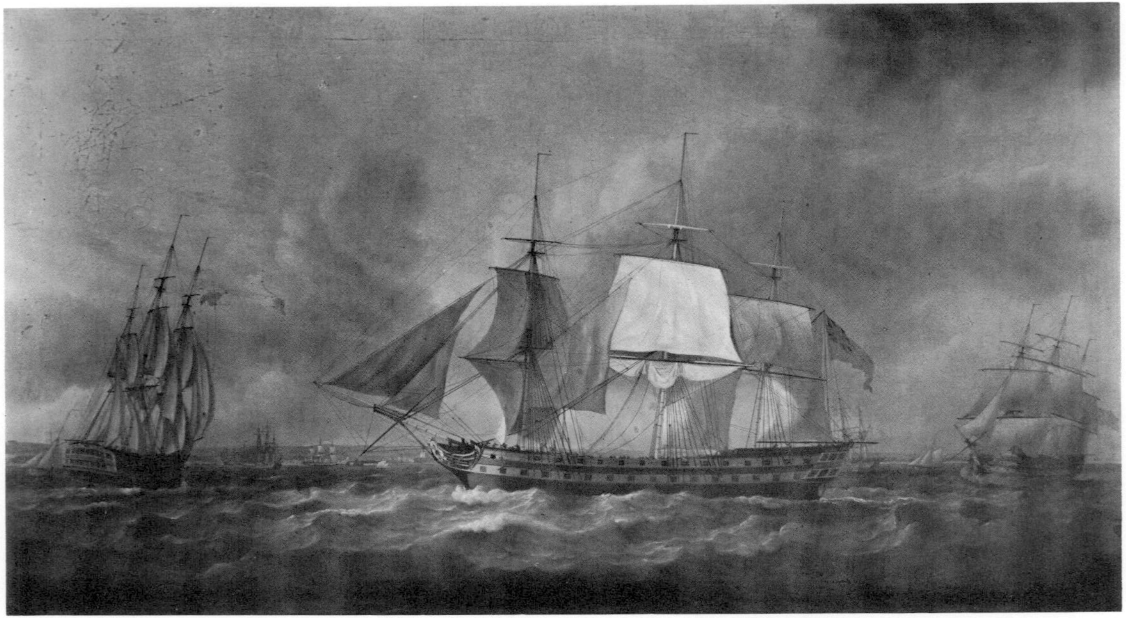

The *Earl of Abergavenny,* East Indiaman, off Southsea. John Wordsworth became Captain of the *Abergavenny* in 1801 and perished with her in the shipwreck off Portland on February 5, 1805. (Reproduced from a painting by T. Luny in the India Office Collection, with permission of the Secretary of State for Commonwealth Affairs.)

The Letters of John Wordsworth

Edited by Carl H. Ketcham

Professor of English, University of Arizona

Cornell University Press

Ithaca, New York

First published 1969

Library of Congress Catalog Card Number: 68-8705

PRINTED IN THE UNITED STATES OF AMERICA
BY KINGSPORT PRESS

Acknowledgments

In preparing this book I have received generous and gracious help for which I am sincerely appreciative. The project was initially made possible by the kindness of Professor Basil Willey, the Trustees of the Wordsworth Library at Grasmere, and the Cornell Library Board, who gave me permission to publish the Grasmere collection of John Wordsworth's letters and related family papers as microfilmed by Cornell. Mrs. John Moorman and Mr. George Healey gave me indispensable advice and encouragement at the start of my undertaking, and Mr. Healey's staff in the Department of Rare Books, Cornell University Library, made a summer's work in Ithaca pleasant and rewarding. I should also like to thank the following librarians and their assistants, all of whom went out of their way to make my task easier: Miss Nesta Clutterbuck, Wordsworth Library; Mr. B. C. Jones, Archivist, Joint Archives Committee for Cumberland and Westmorland and the City of Carlisle; Miss Joan C. Lancaster, Assistant Keeper, India Office Records; and Mr. J. A. C. West, Chief Librarian, Weymouth Public Library.

I am indebted to Mr. L. Brownson of Ambleside, who made arrangements for me to examine Ann Tyson's account book; and to the Chairman of the Governors and the Trustees of Hawkshead Grammar School for permission to publish excerpts from these accounts. A person who wishes to remain anonymous has kindly allowed me to quote from certain Wordsworth family papers. Unpublished Crown-copyright material in the India Office Records transcribed in this book and the photograph of the *Earl of Abergavenny* appear by permission of the Secretary of State for Commonwealth Affairs.

Mr. Reginald Riggs, Station Officer, Her Majesty's Coastguard, Portland Bill, Dorsetshire, furnished technical information. The advice of Professor Chester L. Shaver of Oberlin College was most helpful, and I have found his recent edition of the early letters of William and Dorothy Wordsworth useful in making several identifications. Mr. Frank P. Rand's study, *Wordsworth's Mariner Brother,* has helped me to interpret in one or two places John Wordsworth's handwriting.

I am also grateful to the University of Arizona Alumni Association, the English Department, and the Graduate College of the University of Arizona for support that enabled me to secure much-needed research and clerical help. Finally, I owe special thanks to Professor Mark Reed of the University of North Carolina and to Professors A. Laurence Muir, Richard Hosley, and Oliver Sigworth of the University of Arizona, who read my manuscript and offered valuable criticism and comment.

CARL H. KETCHAM

Tucson, Arizona
August 1968

Contents

Illustrations

The Letters of John Wordsworth

In the summer of 1966 I took the bus from Weymouth to Portland and climbed the hill behind the town, looking for a point from which I could see the Shambles lightship. Halfway up I stopped in a pub to ask directions. To the old man who told me the way, I explained that I was interested in a shipwreck that had taken place on the Shambles in 1805.

"Ah," he said, "the *Earl of Abergavenny!*"

"That's right," I said.

"Captain Wordsworth!"

"Right."

"Yes." Then, after a reflective pause: "You know—he had a brother who was a poet."

C. H. K.

Introduction

On Monday, February 11, 1805, William Wordsworth and his wife Mary returned from a walk to find a visitor at their Grasmere cottage. Mrs. Wordsworth's sister, Sara Hutchinson, who had been staying with a friend at Kendal, seventeen miles to the southeast, had appeared unannounced after a rapid and anxious journey. She brought with her a letter that she had intercepted at the Ambleside post office on her way. It was a brief, rather businesslike note, written by William's brother Richard, a London attorney.

Staple Inn
7th Febry 1805.

My dear Brother,

It is with the most painful concern that I inform you of the Loss of the Ship Abergavenny, off Weymouth last night.

I am acquainted with but few of the particulars of this melancholy Event. I am told that a great number of Persons have perished, and that our Brother John is amongst that number. Mr. Joseph Wordsworth is amongst those who have been saved. The Ship struck against a Rock, & went to the Bottom—

You will impart this to Dorothy in the best manner you can,

& remember me most affly to her, & your wife, believe me your's most sincerely,

R^{d} Wordsworth [1]

Sara, who must have read of the disaster in a Kendal paper, had hurried to be with Mary, William, and Dorothy— "to be of use in the house and to comfort us," as William wrote; in the midst of her distress she had thought to stop and ask for the letter that she knew Richard must have sent. Her comfort was welcome. For months the Town End cottage was a house of mourning. "God keep the rest of us together!" William wrote to Richard; "The set is now broken." "We . . . console each other by weeping together," he wrote to his brother Christopher two days later. Again, a month after the wreck: "Dorothy though not ill is very thin and weak. . . . We are almost heart-broken." On March 7, Dorothy was still too miserable to write and thank Sir Walter Scott for his gift of *The Lay of the Last Minstrel.* Eight days later she spoke of her frequent tears and of the family's weeping together. On May 4, though she could think of John "with pleasure as no longer of this world," her letter about him was interrupted by tears. William, after finishing *The Prelude* in late May, was haunted by depression at the thought of the pleasure he would have had in showing the manuscript to John. On June 8, at the mountain tarn where he and John had parted from each other on the day John left Grasmere for the last time, William was overcome with "floods of tears" as he wrote the "Elegiac Verses in Memory of My Brother." "My tears *will* flow by fits," wrote Dorothy at the end of November; and she was near weeping when she mentioned John in a letter on Christmas Day.[2] As late as 1808, William could still not bear the thought of living near the sea.[3] John's friends and acquaintances were also bitterly grieved at his death. Southey came to Grasmere and wept with William and Dorothy.[4] Charles Lamb wrote of the pain and confusion with which he received the news.[5] Coleridge, hearing it "abruptly & in the very painfullest way possible in a public Company" at his employer's mansion on Malta, was assisted home in a state of near-collapse and remained ill for a fortnight after.[6]

The effects on Wordsworth of this prolonged and shattering grief have been traced repeatedly in his poems, in his philosophy, in the history of his creative imagination. If, as many believe, his brother's death was indeed a turning-point in his career, we need to know as well as we can the causes of his agony. What was distinctive about John Wordsworth's life and character that so endeared him to the set which was broken by his death? William and Dorothy give us many of the answers in their letters, and William in the series of elegiac poems into which he transmuted his longing and pain. But the poems and letters were writen mostly after the shock of the tragedy and colored by intense suffering. *De mortuis* is a sound basis for a tribute, but an uncertain one for scholarship. These considerations have led Professor R. C. Townsend to suggest that William, in the elegies, virtually shaped John in his own changing image (see note 203). Our question, then, becomes a double one: why was John's loss so deeply felt, and to what extent was William's praise of his brother justified?

Fortunately, the evidence needed for at least a partial solution to these problems is available, and has been available for some time to scholars who have had access to the collection of John's letters deposited in the Dove Cottage Library and microfilmed by Cornell University. This collection, assembled, annotated, and partly transcribed by William Wordsworth's grandson Gordon Graham Wordsworth, begins with the year 1792, when John, already an experienced sailor at nineteen, was between voyages to China with the East India Company; it ends with two letters written on January 31, 1805, five days before his death.[7] It is uneven in its coverage of John's career, for it contains no letters from his long Eastern voyages. However, the main facts of these voyages are contained in several ships' logs or journals preserved in the India Office Library. With the help of these logs, family letters and accounts, and John's own letters (most of them published here for the first time in their complete form), we can piece together a fairly continuous story of John's activities through much of his lifetime. More important, we can gain some insight into the personality and way of thought of this shy sailor, the "*silent* Poet" whose devotion to William and his career was so bitterly missed when it came tragically to an end.

John Wordsworth was born in Cockermouth, Cumberland, at 4 A.M. on December 4, 1772,[8] the fourth of five children and the third son. On January 6, 1773, he was baptized in the parish church.[9] His father, for whom he was named, was an attorney who, much to his family's later disadvantage, served as agent to Sir James Lowther, future Earl of Lonsdale. Sir James, in local folklore that rested on bitter experience, was known as the "Bad Earl." Mary Wordsworth's Memoir calls him a "strange Being";[10] one form his strangeness took, in addition to a fondness for dueling and crooked politics, was an aversion to paying debts—"acting," Charles Lamb commented, "in conformity with a plan my lord had taken up in early life of making everybody unhappy."[11] Among his unpaid obligations was a debt of £4625 owed to John Wordsworth, Senior—the "Lowther debt," which figures so largely in the letters of William and Dorothy. Other, unpublished family papers bear witness to the expertness of the Earl's legal staff in evasion of subpoenas, delaying tactics, counter-charges. Lord Lonsdale played his slippery game to the end, and died in 1802 without having paid a penny of the debt.

The stress created by Lowther's eccentricities, however, was not felt by the Wordsworth children for several years. They spent their early childhood in the large, many-windowed house in Cockermouth supplied by Sir James for his agent. Behind the house a terrace overlooked the Derwent. Not far away were the enchanting ruins of Cockermouth Castle, and below it a small millrace where John, like William, must often have "made one long bathing of a summer's day." [12] ("He was an excellent swimmer," William wrote after John's death in the icy water of Weymouth Bay.) [13] We do not know where John learned to read and write—possibly from his mother, though she died before he was six, or from Mrs. Anne Birkett, the old schoolmistress who taught William when the children went to visit their grandparents at Penrith.[14] John and his younger brother Christopher began the rudiments of Latin as pupils of the Rev. Mr. Gilbanks of Cockermouth, when John was seven.[15] John remained at Cockermouth through 1781, then, in January, 1782, joined his two older brothers in the ancient grammar school at Hawkshead in northern Lancashire.[16]

Hawkshead Grammar School deserved the excellent reputation it had enjoyed since its founding by Archbishop Sandys two centuries before. Most of the boys who gathered around the long desks in the plain stone oblong of its one building with its curious sundial set over the door, were destined for the Universities, teaching, or the Church. Hawkshead trained them well in the classics and mathematics; William, indeed, explained his lack of achievement at Cambridge partly by the fact that his Hawkshead training had put him so far ahead of his University classmates that he got into idle habits. John's letters show no direct evidence of his classical studies, but he learned to write his own language pointedly, though casually.

Like his brothers, John boarded with old Ann Tyson, who, during most of John's stay at Hawkshead, lived in a cottage at Colthouse, about half a mile from Hawkshead near one end of Esthwaite Lake. Ann, a carpenter's wife, was his landlady, cook, nurse, and in many ways a substitute for the mother he had lost so early. She saw to the boys' clothes, provided their food and an occasional special treat of cake or wine, and cared for them when they were sick (their father's account book includes a payment for "additional trouble" during an illness of Richard's).[17] The entries in her ledgers during John's stay at Colthouse show her devoted attention to his needs and wants. His birthday was celebrated with an outlay of 1*s.* 6*d.;* she bought him garters, "a ribon," and velvet (perhaps for a school uniform); she had his hair cut, got him a "Cop[y] bok" for school, provided three cakes.[18] Her house was a home for John and his brothers; years later, William recalled how the "old Dame, so kind and motherly" had welcomed his return from Cambridge with "a parent's pride" and some loving tears (*Prelude* IV, 27–29).

Life in the Tysons' cottage was easygoing and comfortable. Around the peat fire in winter or at the stone table under the pine tree in summer, there were endless games of tick-tack-toe, or loo and whist played with the remnants of a battered pack. Free to roam as they pleased, the boys had for their playground a singularly lovely corner of northwest England. John probably took no more conscious notice of natural beauty at first than his elder brother, who learned to love it partly because of its association with the "glad animal movements" of his sports and games. But John, like William, was unknowingly storing up images which were to haunt him in later life, when, "pacing to and fro the vessel's deck" [19] in a calm, he "heard / The tones of waterfalls, and inland sounds / Of caves and trees" or "Below him, in the bosom of the deep, / Saw mountains; saw the forms of sheep that grazed / On verdant hills—with dwellings among trees, / And shepherds." [20] Meanwhile it was a good country for an active boy to grow up in. The lakes provided boating, fishing, swimming, skating; on the hills there were nutting expeditions, birds'-nesting, trapping, hare-and-hounds. Occasionally an expedition to Windermere brought more sophisticated pleasures—strawberries and cream and a game of bowls on the hotel lawn. It speaks well for the Hawkshead masters and Ann Tyson's supervision that the boys came away with as much book knowledge as they did. William spoke of himself later as somewhat spoiled by his freedom, "ill-tutored for captivity" and not particularly "prompt / To in-door study." [21] John had the same propensities, and suffered for them: "Our poor John," Dorothy recalled in 1807, "was called a dunce because, poor Boy, he loved his own solitary dreamings, wanderings with his fishing rod, or social Boyish sports, better than his master's tasks." [22]

During his second year at Hawkshead another family

tragedy put an end to the home at Cockermouth. Indeed, John never had a true home again. At best the Wordsworth children had seen too little of their father, who was often away on business. (Later memories suggest that their relationship with him, in spite of frequent separations, was close and affectionate: because of John's "lonely and retired habits," which seem to have been with him almost from the beginning, his father nicknamed him the Ibex, "the shyest of all the beasts.") [23] In a familiar passage in the *Prelude,* William described how, at Christmas 1783, he climbed to a lookout point to watch eagerly for the horses which were to carry him and his brothers back to their father's house.[24] It was their last journey there: less than ten days after his sons came home, John Wordsworth Sr. died of an illness that followed a winter night he had spent, lost, on the open fells. On January 2, 1784,[25] Richard, William, and John walked in a heartbroken procession behind his coffin as it was carried through a whirling snowstorm to Cockermouth churchyard. The household was dissolved and their father's effects sold. Uncle Richard came from Whitehaven to attend the sale, where he apparently bought a watch and a silver coffee pot. Family sentiment, however, did not keep him from charging the estate for travel expenses to Cockermouth and for his loss in two guineas from his dead brother's pocket that proved to be short weight.[26]

Holidays from then on were times of misery for the young Wordsworths. Their mother's parents, the Cooksons of Penrith, felt it their duty to provide a home for their grandchildren; John and his brothers lived with them during summer vacations, and sister Dorothy, who had been staying with her mother's cousin in Halifax, joined the household in 1787. Possibly a houseful of children was too much for the old people. They seem to have been a narrow sort at best, unable to resist treating the young Wordsworths as poor relations. Their son Christopher generally ignored his nephews (especially William, to whom he had taken a dislike), and the servants were quick to follow their employers' lead by scolding the children and taunting them with their dependence and lack of fortune. Dorothy (who to be sure had a spirit which never took an affront lightly) wrote of constant lectures from her grandfather, insults from the servants ("my Brs can not even get a pair of shoes cleaned without James's telling them they require as much waiting upon as any *Gentlemen*"), and petty tyrannies from "Uncle Kit," who once left the boys at school for a week after the holidays began because they had not specifically asked him to send horses for them. "Many a time," Dorothy wrote, "have W[illia]m, J[ohn], C[hristopher], and myself shed tears together, tears of the bitterest sorrow, we all of us, each day, feel more sensibly the loss we sustained when we were deprived of our parents. . . . [We] always finish our conversations which generally take a melancholy turn, with wishing we had a father and a home." [27]

We do not know exactly when John decided to follow the sea. Another John Wordsworth, a cousin on his father's side and some eighteen years his senior, was already well established with the East India Company, where personal influence was a sure means to advancement. John Robinson, M.P., his father's cousin, had valuable influence as well. John's experience at Hawkshead had probably convinced him that the University was not for him ("He is not so bright as either W[illia]m or Christopher," Dorothy wrote), especially if it led to the Church, the other profession in which his family had influence; "churchiness" was what he liked least about his brother Christopher and uncle William in later years. He was active, a sportsman, with good common sense and no fear of loneliness—all in all, as Dorothy said, "well calculated for the profession he has chosen." [28] Christopher Cookson's accounts show all four brothers together at Hawkshead in December, 1785, when a Mr. Mingay was paid for giving them dancing lessons.[29] However, by the summer of 1787, John's course was decided. He returned to Hawkshead with William and Christopher for a half-term beginning August, 1787. William remained till October, when he went off to Penrith for a visit before entering Cambridge. John and Christopher stayed until the Christmas holidays, which they spent at Whitehaven,[30] and this was apparently the end of John's formal schooling.

He seems to have studied navigation for a short time with a Mr. Wood, whose bill was paid on February 24,[31] before sailing for Barbados—[32] his first experience on shipboard. He had returned by August 6, when his Uncle Richard paid freight for his chest and gave him a guinea. While ashore he apparently studied navigation again, then left on a voyage to Jamaica; a bill for cheese and tea paid October 2 suggests the stocking of his sea chest with some personal comforts, and his sea clothes were washed and his shoes mended at about the same time.[33]

Dorothy expected his return in March or April, 1789, and he seems to have arrived on schedule: Uncle Richard paid freight for his sea chest on April 29.[34] Though the records are not entirely clear at this point, he was probably at sea again before the end of the summer, this time bound for America.[35] What ports he touched and what his days ashore were like we do not know, but his waterfront experiences left him with a deep dislike of the country and everyone in it. "It is a most detestable place," he wrote, long afterward, to Mary Hutchinson.

He had returned to England by October, and joined his brother Richard, who had come to London earlier that year as a clerk in a law firm. Together they set out on a visit to Forncett Rectory in Norfolk,[36] where, in an old, high-windowed building at the end of an avenue of lime trees, Dorothy Wordsworth shared a home with her uncle, the Reverend William Cookson, and his bride of a year. It was a joyous reunion, but a brief one; Richard's court sessions drew near, and in mid-October the brothers returned to London.[37] John had received welcome news: his cousin Captain John Wordsworth had found a berth for him in his ship, the *Earl of Abergavenny*—John's first in the series of posts with the East India Company that led him finally to the rank of commander. Preparations for the voyage occupied him during the late fall. He still depended on his guardians for his sea clothes and the few belongings his sea chest would hold, for his wages had hardly paid for his extras on shipboard. Prudent Uncle Kit sent thirty pounds to buy him "necessarys" for this trip, but (mindful perhaps that John was only seventeen) asked Richard to see to it that the money was spent not by John, but by the Captain.[38]

There was another family gathering at Christmas, when William, then in his third year at Cambridge, came down for the holidays on what may have been his first visit to London. The brothers probably shared Richard's chambers, and John, the experienced Londoner, eagerly led William out on a pedestrian tour of the town. Much to John's annoyance, however, William spotted a copy of Bowles's *Fourteen Sonnets* at a bookseller's, bought them, and insisted on reading them as he walked, ignoring his brother's commentary on the city's wonders, until at London Bridge William lodged himself firmly in a niche and refused to move on until he had finished the pamphlet.[39] In retrospect we can understand his absorption; but to John this practical demonstration of Bowles's influence was only a puzzle and a nuisance.

William was probably still in town when Midshipman Wordsworth was ordered on board his cousin's ship. The *Earl of Abergavenny*—pronounced, as John often spells it, Abergāny[40]—was a three-masted vessel of nearly 1200 tons, bound for Bombay and China on her maiden voyage. For John, with his love of wandering, the prospect of a journey halfway round the world must have been sheer magic, but in fact this voyage, as voyages went, turned out to be tame enough. Having left her first moorings in the river on January 17, 1790, the *Abergavenny* sailed with the *Osterley* on the 30th. On March 13, her log notes, "Cross'd the Line, with the usual Ceremonies." She reached Bombay Harbor on June 7.[41] On August 8th she sailed again; on the 25th she stopped briefly at Penang. A crewman was washed overboard in "a violent Tuffoon" on September 26. October 3 found her at Whampoa, the anchorage for Canton and the farthest point of the voyage. When her English and Indian goods and her silver had been unloaded, and her westbound cargo of cottons, tea, and raw silk had been bargained for with her officially-appointed Chinese merchant and stowed aboard, the *Abergavenny* began her homeward journey on February 3, 1791. The next day she ran aground on the second bar (not a rare occurrence under the guidance of a Chinese pilot) but got off again in a few hours and on March 20 sailed from Macao Roads with the Fleet. After a halt for water and livestock at St. Helena in early July, she anchored in the Thames on August 19.[42] On September 29 John drew his wages—£21 19*s.* 10*d.* after deductions,[43] for a voyage of over twenty months.

No letters written by John on any of his Eastern trips have survived. Except for a reliable post from St. Helena, the sending of private letters apparently depended upon encounters with homeward-bound ships. It was by some such means that Richard got John's letter of February 21, 1790, saying he was "perfectly contented & happy" on the *Abergavenny*.[44] There is no record of further letters from him on the voyage. On October 9, 1791, Dorothy mentioned his arrival in England; she had heard that he "is grown a very tall handsome man." [45] In November his Uncle Kit complained to Richard, "I am surpris'd your Bro^{r} John does not think it worth his while to write to either his Grandmother or me, I must confess I look upon it as a very great piece of Ingratitude." [46] John, who like his brothers detested routine letter-writing, seems to have been busy trying to get a berth on an Indiaman; in early December he expected to sail with the *Thetis* in the spring.[47] Uncle Kit and John's grandmother recovered from their sense of his ingratitude sufficiently for the latter to send him a present of £100, to "be laid out in a frugal manner in fitting him out & purchasing a small venture to take with him to China." [48] But his plans fell through, and the *Thetis* sailed without him.

Probably having found that he could accomplish nothing more by staying in London, John went north at the end of the year for a visit of four months at Forncett Rectory, with Dorothy, his Aunt and Uncle Cookson, and their growing family. (Ten years later, on another visit, he was to record his impressions of the young Cooksons, who had appeared almost annually from 1790 through 1797.) He left Norfolk on April 30, 1792,[49] intending to stay in London a short while, then to go to Whitehaven, a busy port in Cumberland, where he would ship for the West Indies or America. Dorothy sent after him a parcel of silk which he had left behind—evidently a gift for his relatives in the North.[50] In early May he spent three or four days with his mother's cousins the Misses Griffith at Newcastle; [51] then he went to Penrith, sending his sea chest on to Whitehaven (Uncle Richard charged the expense to his father's estate) [52] while he visited his uncle Thomas Myers and his Uncle Kit. He found his grandmother Cookson, Uncle Kit's mother, seriously ill; she died on June 11,[53] and not until July 25 is there any record of his finally going to Whitehaven. Even then the trip was apparently only a call, partly for business purposes, on his cousin Captain Wordsworth, who was between voyages; after a few days he met his brother Christopher at the home of Captain Wordsworth's sister Mrs. Smith, and the two brothers went off together for a seaside visit at Rampside, again staying with one of the Captain's sisters. Then followed a jaunt over the hills with Christopher, who was returning to Hawkshead, and at last a cross-country journey back to Whitehaven. Richard may have been right when he commented on August 27, "I suppose that John will not take his intended Voyage from Whitehaven as he has deferred it so long." [54] We know, however, that at some time John sailed from Whitehaven and spent two months on the island of São Miguel in the Azores.[55] Quite possibly this voyage occupies a gap in the record of his movements between the late summer of 1792 and early 1793.[56]

John was in attendance when the *Abergavenny*, after

undergoing the usual repairs, came out of drydock on March 16; he boarded her again on April 23, and remained aboard after May 6. In the intervals he was preparing, as fifth mate, to take advantage of the opportunities for private trade allowed to the officers by the Company. His wages were only forty-five shillings a month, "by no means adequate," he explained to Uncle Kit, "to the expences which must necessarily accrue on the voyage." The real means of success in the Company's maritime service lay in the precious cargo weight which was allotted each officer according to rank, and which, if he had capital, he might fill as he saw fit (within Company rules) for trade on his own account. The fifth mate's share must have been small indeed, but in the years of John's later voyages a second mate could take a maximum of six tons, the first mate eight, and the captain's allotment of fifty-six tons [57] might, if the markets were good, make him a rich man after a very few voyages. Dorothy, at John's request, agreed to lend him £100 given her by her grandmother Cookson. The *Abergavenny* had left her first anchorage in the Thames before the draft arrived, but Richard had probably advanced John the money. On May 22, 1793, the East India Fleet sailed under convoy from Spithead.

They encountered cold weather south of the Line; Captain Wordsworth fortified his crew with a ration of boiled wheat, sweetened with molasses, essence of malt, and a little brandy. Since John had been unable to lay in trade goods with Dorothy's money, he paid £79 16*s.* 7*d.* at Manila for a bag of 371.4 Spanish dollars; these could be sold at a good profit in China, where they were an important supplement to the inconvenient Chinese currency.[58] For the return voyage from Canton he bought nankeen cloth, chinaware, and "China grass" [59] (ramie, a fiber plant). The *Abergavenny* left the Boca Tigris, at the mouth of the Pearl River below Canton, on March 17, 1794, and anchored at Northfleet in the Thames on September 11.[60]

Richard wrote on October 13 that John had "fully expected" to see William in town.[61] William had indeed been planning to come to London to start a monthly publication with his friend William Mathews. They had both had second thoughts, however, as the date agreed on for beginning drew near; and at the time of John's arrival William was in the North, first on a visit to the Barkers at Rampside, then in attendance on his sick friend Raisley Calvert, to whose legacy he was soon to owe the beginnings of his independence. (In November he was still longing for London, and wrote in a most un-Wordsworthian way to Mathews that "cataracts and mountains, are good occasional society, but they will not do for constant companions.") [62] John, meanwhile, was going back and forth to his ship at Greenhithe, seeing none of his family except Richard, who was handling his accounts; at year's end his capital in Richard's books stood at £168 5*s.* 4*d.*[63] The resources of Eastern trade were still untapped.

The *Abergavenny,* now besieged with floating ice in the Thames as the last details of her voyage neared completion, was soon to be sold to the Government; her replacement, a heavier vessel of the same name, would not be launched for more than a year (*EY* 122 n.; WP). In late February 1795 John drew his wages of £41 11*s.* 8*d.*[64] About this time William finally arrived in London.[65] Almost certainly the brothers met, though no record of their meeting survives; John, however, could spare little time between ships. On March 11, he first went on board the *Osterley,* an East Indiaman, as fourth mate—a promotion that cost him eight guineas for new uniforms—[66] and on April 22 dropped downriver on the way to the Downs and Portsmouth. A month later the combined East India, West India, and Mediterranean fleets set sail together. The *Osterley* was carrying soldiers, part of an expedition to the Cape of Good Hope, which the English had undertaken to hold against the French on behalf of the Prince of Orange. Landing and provisioning these troops occupied several weeks. One incident in what was otherwise a routine operation has a certain ominousness, if read in the light of later events. The log of the *Osterley* for September 14 records without comment: "PM Mr Wordsworth 4th Officer who had charge of the Longboat to the Camp at Musinburg Island provisions for the Army, return'd with an Account of the Boat being drove onshore in the Gale & beat to pieces."

The *Osterley* was at Whampoa from March 7 until June 19, 1796. On July 5 she sailed with the fleet from Macao Harbor on a return voyage of seven months, anchoring in Long Reach on February 14, 1797.[67] John Wordsworth had already left her, perhaps by the pilot boat on February 8, for on the 10th he was aboard his next ship, the *Duke of Montrose,* as second mate (he was formally approved for the position on March 1st).[68] He seems to have made little profit from his private trade on the *Osterley,* and his wages (signed for by Richard, since John could not leave his ship) were only £51 11*s.* 3*d.*[69] On April 26 he was on his way again, and again just missed receipt of a loan of £100, this time from his Uncle Kit.[70] He probably received it in the Downs, where the *Duke of Montrose* lay at anchor from April 28 to May 7 and where he wrote to Richard expressing his anxiety at having had no letters from William or Dorothy.[71]

Meanwhile, ugly rumors were spreading among his ship's crew. The *Duke of Montrose,* said the men, was unseaworthy, a leaky tub that was likely to drown them all. When it came time for her to sail from Portsmouth, on June 5, the crew gathered together and, "soberly and in decent deportment," refused to weigh anchor until the leak was stopped. Captain Patrick Burt, probably surprised at the restraint of a gang scavenged from the waterfront (John later said one of his own crews was "only *trash*") tried to argue with them. When that failed, he attempted to sail with the help of the passengers (we can imagine the crew's comments on their efforts) but had to give up and anchor again. Discipline on the Indiamen was usually a simple matter of flogging or clapping in irons, but in this case the Commodore refused to sanction coercion. Instead the Company's surveyor came aboard and announced that the leak was unimportant, a little over an inch an hour. Twenty "disaffected" and "refractory" seamen were sent ashore. In July, after several false starts baffled by contrary weather, the *Duke of Montrose* and the rest of the East India Fleet worked their way into the open Channel, only to be met by a strong breeze from the southwest that drove them into Tor Bay, on the southeast coast of Devon. There they waited during almost eight weeks of westerly winds, finally setting out again on September 22.

The leak had not been stopped, however; with the stress of the ship's motion it increased to thirteen inches an hour, and the crew came near to open rebellion. When matters reached such a point "that the Petty Officers were become in constant dread of Assassination in the

Night," three ringleaders were sent aboard the Senior Commander's ship, where they could be guarded by the King's troops. That ended the threat of mutiny, but the leak continued (reaching 19 inches per hour at one point) until the ship, after stopping at Madras, entered the yards at Calcutta, where she could be thoroughly caulked. More than seven months later, on November 3, 1798, she dropped downriver to Diamond Harbor. She did not put out to sea till February, 1799. John managed somehow to get a letter to Richard before May 15, reporting that he was well and happy.[72] After spending ten days at St. Helena in late May, the *Duke of Montrose* anchored in Long Reach on August 2.[73]

John's absence (reckoning from the time he left London) had spanned an eventful period in the lives of William and Dorothy: their move from Racedown to Alfoxden in July, 1797, the Tintern Abbey visit and the *Lyrical Ballads* in 1798, their bitterly cold winter in Germany, 1798–1799, and their stay at Sockburn-on-Tees beginning in April or May, 1799. Sockburn farm was the home of Thomas Hutchinson, his brother George, and his sisters Sara, Joanna, and Mary. Another sister, Margaret, had died in 1796; the oldest brother, John, lived in Stockton, and another brother, Henry, followed the sea. The Hutchinsons and the Wordsworths had first known each other in Mrs. Birkett's "dame school," which William had attended as a small boy during visits to his grandparents at Penrith. Dorothy had renewed her friendship with the Hutchinson girls when she came to live in the grandparents' home in 1787, and William came to know Mary well during his summer vacations from Cambridge in 1788 and 1789. The lives of the sisters grew curiously intertwined with those of the Wordsworth circle. Joanna is the subject of one of William's more striking poems. Sara was the object of Coleridge's muddled, hopeless love. Mary, of course, became William's wife in 1802; but both she and Sara were involved with John Wordsworth in ways that must claim our attention further on.

Richard had failed to mention to anyone that John had come home; this negligence annoyed Dorothy, who only heard by chance of her brother's return. "Why," she asked Richard, "did you not write to inform us of his arrival and where to address to him?" [74] John, meanwhile, drew his pay of £93 4*s.* 8*d.* on October 4,[75] and on the 6th [76] went north to his Uncle Kit's estate, Newbiggin Hall near Penrith, leaving his business affairs in Richard's hands as usual. His trading profit on the voyage was some £400 [77]—modest enough in view of his expectations and the amount of capital he was to be handling in a few years, but a comfortable sum considered as two years' earnings. Shortly after John's arrival at Newbiggin, his uncle died; the burial took place on October 17, and John stayed long enough to hear the reading of the will.[78]

William, who had been no favorite with his uncle, had rather pointedly ignored the funeral. He was, in fact, involved with a long-anticipated project—introducing Coleridge to the Lake District. Coleridge arrived at Sockburn with Cottle, the printer of the *Lyrical Ballads,* but Wordsworth had planned a tour on foot and horseback, and the rheumatic Cottle proved unequal to the damp and the exercise: on October 30 he left the others, who traveled on from Greta Bridge and spent the night at Temple Sowerby. From the landlady at the inn Wordsworth learned, apparently quite by chance, that John was staying at Newbiggin. He sent over a note. John appeared, looking "very well" (Wordsworth's somewhat laconic comment after a separation of at least four years).[79] Learning for the first time about the proposed tour, John decided to join it for part of the route.

The three men tramped south, dined at Barton with the Wordsworths' uncle by marriage Thomas Myers, and slept at Bampton. The next day took them along the edge of Hawes Water and by way of Long Sleddale to Kentmere. On November 2 they came within the familiar range of the brothers' expeditions from school: skirting Windermere to the ferry below Bowness, they found themselves only an hour's brisk walk from Esthwaite Lake, their old schoolhouse, and the whitewashed church which sat "like a thronèd Lady" [80] above Hawkshead village. At Hawkshead they spent the night, and the following morning turned north to Grasmere. They visited the Rydal waterfall on the way, but this "very magnificent" [81] bit of Lakeland scenery was rather spoiled, for Coleridge at least, by a servant of Sir Michael le Fleming, who came after them to reprove them for having walked in front of Sir Michael's house.[82] They passed the night at Robert Newton's inn opposite the church. Monday, November 4, was spent in the vicinity of Grasmere; and it may have been on this day that William first conceived the idea which was to influence so profoundly the whole course of his life. "You will think my plan a mad one," he wrote to Dorothy, "but I have thought of building a house there by the Lake side. . . . There is a small house at Grasmere empty which perhaps we may take . . . but of this we will speak." Both Coleridge and John had encouraged the project. Coleridge "was much struck with Grasmere and its neighbourhood." [83] John, it seems, had from the beginning wanted to devote his own resources to William's future. As Dorothy had written in 1787, "John poor fellow! says that he shall have occasion for very little, two hundred pounds will be enough to fit him out, and he should wish Wm to have the rest for his education, as he has a wish to be a Lawyer if his health will permit, and it will be very expensive."[84] Later the opportunity to assist William in his poetry was one of the chief motives of John's voyages. "He encouraged me," William wrote, "to persist in the plan of life which I had adopted; I will work for you was his language and you shall attempt to do something for the world."[85] Now at Grasmere his offer of help was immediate and practical: since William had found a site that he liked, John would give him £40 to buy the ground. In the end, construction costs proved too high, the plan to build was abandoned, and it was to the small empty house (now called Dove Cottage) that William and Dorothy moved as tenants in late December.

John had left the tour after a day in Grasmere, making his way northeast near Helvellyn and parting with William and Coleridge by Grisedale Tarn, where, several months later, William and Dorothy were to see him for the last time in the Lake District. None of his impressions of the journey have survived. Coleridge, to whom the district was new, recorded in his diary the shades and colors of lakes, trees, mountains, finding shapes in the latter that were human and sometimes obscene.[86] John was less verbal but no less responsive: William called him "a *silent* Poet," and Coleridge was deeply impressed by his sensitivity. "Your Br. John is one of you," he wrote to Dorothy near the close of the tour; "a man who hath solitary usings of his own Intellect, deep in feeling, with a subtle Tact, a swift instinct of Truth & Beauty. He interests me much."[87] John, for his part, was warmly attached to

Coleridge and must have listened with fascination to his flow of talk. Was it perhaps from Coleridge that he learned Aristotle's fundamental account of literary structure, that the action imitated must be complete in itself with a beginning, middle, and end?

We lose sight of John for about two months; probably he returned to Newbiggin. On Christmas Eve Dorothy was expecting him daily at their Grasmere cottage, but he did not arrive until January. The manner of his coming gives us a revealing glimpse of his personality. He knew his visit was expected, and he could have had no fear of too sudden a surprise in appearing, though Dorothy had not seen him for several years; but some overwhelming combination of shyness and strong feeling made him turn away from the cottage door when his hand was already on the latch. He approached twice without finding the courage to enter, and finally sent word of his arrival from the village inn.[88]

It was a dubious beginning, but the visit was a high point in the lives of all of them, and one on which William and Dorothy looked back for comfort in later years. "He loved this fireside," Dorothy wrote; "he paced over this floor in pride before we had been six weeks in the house, exulting within his noble heart that his Father's Children had once again a home together." [89] John's stay lasted eight months. He roamed the country with his fishing rod or worked on small contrivances to make the house more comfortable. "He loved our cottage," said Dorothy; "he helped us to furnish it, and to make the gardens—trees are growing now which he planted." [90] John took the same intense delight in the Grasmere scenery that finds expression in William's poems and Dorothy's journals. "Many a time,' Dorothy wrote, "has he called me out in an evening to look at the moon or stars, or a cloudy sky, or this vale in the quiet moonlight." [91]

Within two days of his arrival at Grasmere, John had traced out a footway among the trees of the fir plantation which from that time on was known in the Wordsworth circle as "John's Grove." It was on what is now the old road to Ambleside, opposite the Wishing Gate. John used to visit it daily, wearing a path through the opening in the trees "By that habitual restlessness of foot / Wherewith a sailor measures o'er and o'er / His short domain upon the Vessels Deck, / —While she is traveling through the dreary seas." [92] William and Dorothy often visited the spot after his departure, to follow his path up to the rock where it ended,[93] and William made it the subject of one of his *Poems on the Naming of Places.* John was furious when some of the firs nearby were cut. He wrote Mary Hutchinson in March 1801, "I wish I had the *monster* that cut them down in *my* ship & I would give him a tight flogging."

Mary would have shared his resentment. She had come to the Grasmere cottage at the end of February for a visit lasting five weeks. During this whole time she and John were steady companions. "John was the first," she wrote, "who led me to everything that I love in this neighborhood." [94] "John used to walk with her every where," Dorothy later recalled, "and they were exceedingly attached to each other." [95] It should not be forgotten that Mary was at Grasmere as a school friend of Dorothy's as well as on William's account. William had been attracted to her in earlier years at Penrith, before his French affair had taught him the meaning of a violent passion. Perhaps Mary figured vaguely in his future plans; but he was a poor man with a sister to support, and Annette Vallon was still on his mind, if not his conscience. Not until late the following year did he finally propose marriage. John, therefore, had been free to speak for himself, had that been his nature. That he did not may be in part because of his shyness, in part because of his schemes for making a quick fortune at sea. Certainly, if he ever felt more than a remote sentimental attachment to anyone, that one was Mary. Evidence in the individual letters is slight—John was not a man to scorch the paper with his passions—but, taken cumulatively, and in the light of what we know about John's reserve, it carries conviction. Mary and no one else, not even Dorothy, is "thou" to him. He reads and re-reads her letters a dozen times a day to be with her; there is nothing she can say that will not interest him. He writes her twice in one day, apologizing for the shortness of the first note; he cannot, he says, spend his time better than in writing to "dearest Mary." He calls on a mutual acquaintance in order to have the pleasure of talking about her. His last note when he is on the point of sailing on his 1801 voyage is to her. Certainly, too, his feeling was in some degree returned. She wrote him often, named part of her garden in his honor, praised his critical judgment. It was William who wrote that "Mary . . . loved John with her whole soul"; Dorothy spoke of her "tender love of John and . . . intimate knowledge of his virtues."[96] It is indeed a pity that her letters to him, except as reflected in his replies, have not survived. One in particular would have taught us, perhaps, the whole story of their relationship: this was the letter she sent to John about a month before William, having settled matters with Annette in France, journeyed north to wed Mary at Brompton Church. For once she broke through John's shyness; too deeply moved to find many words, he spoke his heart to her completely, for the first and last time, in lines from his brother's poem "Michael." "I have been reading your Letter over & over again My dearest Mary till tears have come into my eyes & I known not how to express my[s]elf. Thou ar't [a] kind and dear creature But what ever fate Befal me I shall love [thee] to the last and bear thy memory with me to the grave."

It would probably be a mistake, however, to think that John was deeply embittered, or even in any practical way much changed, by Mary's becoming his "sister," as he called both her and Sara after the marriage. True, he returned from a long voyage to find that William had proposed during his absence. Though nothing in his letters proves that he had not dreamed of Mary as a possible wife, he was not in a position to form definite expectations or ask her to wait for him, and there is no indication of even a tacit understanding between them. His references to Sara, though brief, are almost as affectionate as those to Mary. At most, Mary was *la princesse lointaine,* and to lose her, however poignant the immediate disappointment, involved no betrayal and no acute sense of a final parting: he had not seen her in more than two years. Naturally he stopped writing to her, or if he did write, the letters have not survived. But his letters to Dorothy a month or two later show not the least evidence of heartbreak or of any effort to conceal it.

His last sight of Mary had been in June, 1800 on an excursion that he had made with William during the long visit in Grasmere. They had set off on May 14, with cold pork in their pockets, to explore some of the more curious scenes in northern Yorkshire. We know that they saw the Yordas Cave north of Ingleton, and Gordale Scar, a ravine

300 feet high with waterfalls. Probably they would not have missed visiting the White Star caves near Ingleton, and Malham Cove, a spectacular amphitheatre of rock with the River Aire issuing from its base.[97] But most of their time was spent at Gallow Hill, the farm near Wykeham where Mary and Joanna Hutchinson were keeping house for their brother Tom. Here they stayed between two and three weeks. John probably saw Sara Hutchinson as well as her sisters during this time. The visit was not remarkably long as visits went in those days; we need not speculate about which brother prolonged it on which sister's account. (We do know that John hated the farm itself: "Gallow Hill," he wrote afterward to Dorothy, "is a vile abominable place.") On their return, William went straight home, leaving John to explore the Greta Bridge countryside for a day.

The summer passed with fishing expeditions, picnics, swimming, visits from the Coleridges, cherry-picking, rum-bottling, gathering wildflower seeds for Dorothy's garden. John slept in "a small bed without curtains" in "a small low unceiled room" upstairs, which Dorothy papered with newspapers (they lasted until a few years ago). After his departure she used "Maister John's bed" (in her old servant's phrase) as a sickbed, and after William's marriage, she slept there regularly.[98] Considering the closeness of their quarters, brothers, sister, and guests apparently got on remarkably well, except that John showed "a little hastiness of temper when any thing was done in a clumsy or bungling way, or when improperly contradicted upon occasions of not much importance."[99] This failing went with his profession, Wordsworth thought. (Curiously, John's own clumsiness marks his first appearance in Dorothy's correspondence some years before: he put too much water in her inkwell, so that she produced a series of blots instead of a letter.)[100]

On September 28 came news that the *Earl of Abergavenny* had returned. John lost no time in setting out: on the 29th, William and Dorothy went with him as far as Grisedale Tarn, one of William's and John's favorite fishing spots, where the route from Grasmere, after rounding the foot of the tarn, joins the path down Dollywagon Pike from Helvellyn and begins a winding descent into Patterdale. By the fork in the path they stood together,

> While each into himself descends,
> For that last thought of parting Friends
> That is not to be found.[101]

These lines a century later were carved on the stone that marks the place of parting. Brother and sister watched as John "*hurried* down the stony mountain,"[102] where, between the masses of Dollywagon and Fairfield to left and right, the valley opens out to a glimpse of Ullswater far below. "My heart was right sad," Dorothy wrote, but she "could not help thinking we should see him again, because he was only going to Penrith."[103] It was a comforting illusion for the moment; but John was never to return to Grasmere.

He began at once on ship's business, going from Newbiggin Hall with his Aunt Crackanthorpe (the widow of Uncle Kit, who had dropped the name Cookson in 1792) to see Mr. Parkin, one of the owners of the *Abergavenny*. Then he hurried to London by the mail coach. There was some need to be prompt: Captain John Wordsworth planned to retire from the sea, having made several immensely profitable voyages, and John was to take his place as captain of the *Abergavenny*. A few years earlier the post would have been a marketable commodity; in 1796, however, the East India Company had prohibited the sale of commands (though the practice was easier to prohibit than to stop) and recompensed its captains for the price they had themselves given for their captaincies.[104] It is unlikely that John paid Captain Wordsworth for the position; a bond for £1650 executed between them in early 1801 [105] probably represents a loan from the elder John for his cousin's private trade.

At the beginning of November, arrangements had progressed enough so that John felt free to visit his uncle William and the Cookson family at Forncett Rectory for almost two weeks. On his way back he looked in on his brother Christopher at Cambridge. Christopher had been a Fellow of Trinity since 1798 and was establishing a reputation as a preacher; once a sympathetic companion of William's, he had found the road to preferment in the Church and was beginning to harden in the mold of conventional churchmanship. It is perhaps not surprising that John's visit with him lasted only a day. Returning to London, John began borrowing money for his private trade, and, on free evenings, attending plays. He delighted in comedies, but the huge size of the licensed theatres in London made tragedy an affair of noise and rant that disgusted him. He preferred to read his Shakespeare in the quiet of his cabin on shipboard.

In due course, the East India Company prepared a report on John's background and experience.[106] On January 7, 1801, the Directors accepted and referred to committee a letter from the ship's owners recommending him for the captaincy, and on the same day he was declared "fitly qualified for the Station of Commander" and sworn in, with a solemn warning from the Chairman against illicit trade.[107] On March 4 he took leave of the Court,[108] wearing his new dress uniform—black velvet lapels, buff waistcoat and breeches, light gold embroidery, yellow metal buttons with the Company's crest.[109] Despite his inexperience and shyness, which made dealing with tradesmen difficult, he seemed in a fair way to do well on his voyage. His investment was over nine thousand pounds. Poor Dorothy sent him £80 of her £100 inheritance from Uncle Kit; in return he offered her an allowance of £20 a year. (This, with matching allowances from Christopher and, in the following year, from Richard, should have enabled Dorothy to remain with William without costing him anything, but Richard usually forgot to make the payments.) William sold stock to invest £277 10*s.* in the venture, receiving a bond for his share and Dorothy's.[110] And on August 12, after the *Abergavenny* had sailed, their mother's cousin Robert Griffith of Philadelphia answered an appeal from John with a loan of £200.[111]

In the midst of his own affairs, John, who always thought of himself as a kind of subordinate to William and his creative work, had found time to busy himself about the publication of the *Lyrical Ballads* in a new, two-volume edition (or, more technically, a second edition of the original work plus a new volume). It was to John, rather than the dilatory Richard or the busy publisher Longman, that Sara Hutchinson transmitted a group of letters, mostly dictated by Coleridge but signed by William, to be sent by Longman to a select group of prominent people, together with copies of *Lyrical Ballads* which the letters discreetly advertised. John read the letters with interest and delight, especially the one to Fox, which William had written himself—William "was becoming a most accomplished Courtier," wrote John dryly. He railed at Longman—though not to his face—as a "vile abominable & impudent Jew" for giving only £80 for the copyright, and expostulated with Longman's partner, Rees, about misprints. His attitude toward the sale of the poems was divided between a desire to reassure William (and probably himself) and the realization that the volumes were not going to take London by storm. He wrote that they were sure of a good and steady sale, that Longman would make four or five hundred pounds on them, that they would undoubtedly go into another edition soon, that the second volume had had a "great sale"; but it is clear that the pace at which they were sold disappointed him. He mentioned repeatedly that their popularity must come by degrees, that they could not "meet with their due praise or reward" immediately. Only a few will be pleased with them, he wrote, but "they *will be people of sense*[;] this will have weight—& people who neither understand or wish to understand will buy & praise them." John's strong commercial instinct was an undertone in many of his remarks on his brother's works. Thus in 1802 he praised one of the Bonaparte sonnets but regretted the time invested in work that could never be popular: "I think it is a pity that he [William] should employ himself in that way." He listened anxiously to hear the *Lyrical Ballads* mentioned in company, and unhappily recorded that they were ignored "except I *lug* them in myself."

In the meantime there were beginning to be ominous signs that his captaincy might not, after all, be the easy route to wealth that his cousin had found it. At first John had been reassured that he was to be *"a rich dog";* he rejected an offer to buy his voyage for five thousand pounds, believing that he could make at least six. But the Napoleonic wars were forcing up prices on the trade goods he bought in England. There was a delay in leaving the Thames; the bales he was to take were not ready in time. His first inkling of serious trouble may have come when he reached Portsmouth harbor on March 31 to find the fleet he was supposed to have sailed with just standing out to sea. Too long a wait would mean that the ships which had already sailed for Madras (whose voyages were much more profitable in the first place) would get to China before him, though he was sailing there direct, and spoil his markets. But for week after week he lay in Portsmouth, missing a favorable wind, with no explanation from London as to why his dispatches did not come. He did not sail until May 19, protected against the French by a 74-gun warship.

The *Abergavenny* was herself in effect a privateer, carrying thirty-two guns (she could have mounted seventy if there had been crew enough to man them) and provided with letters of marque authorizing her to capture French merchantmen. During the voyage the guns were several times run out when a strange sail was sighted, but there was no actual engagement. She put in at Rio de Janeiro for water, beef, greens, and rice, then sailed for Penang, where John bought pepper, tin, and betel nut. On January 25, 1802, she reached Macao, and proceeded upriver to remain for two months. John went to Canton twice during his stay. Shore leaves for John, however, seem to have been humdrum affairs, if we can trust his own statement that he disliked *"dashing* on shore" with his fellow commanders. In any case he was luckier than two minor officers of the *Ponsborne,* who in 1781 were thrown overboard from a river boat bound for Canton because they "insisted on having more Girls brought them"— [112] a phrase which gives some idea of what shore leave usually meant.

John's trips to the city were probably hopeless efforts to stave off economic disaster. By 1800 the bottom had dropped out of the woolens market at Canton. Woolen goods were sold at an 11 per cent loss that year,[113] and the price seems not to have mended much by 1802. We know that at least part of John's private trade was in woolens, for late in 1802 he was fined £210 for "smuggling" camlets—that is, importing for his own trade what was supposed to be a Company monopoly. His net loss on outward and homeward voyages together apparently amounted to several thousand pounds.[114]

He left the ship at Gravesend on September 11, 1802,[115] and hurried to London for a conference with Richard. Dorothy and William, by good luck, were in London, too, returning from a month at Calais, where they had gone for a last interview with Annette Vallon before William's marriage.[116] They met Richard and John in the Temple Court, "walking backwards and forwards by the light of the moon and the lamps." Of John, Dorothy wrote, "He was grown fat and looked very handsome," but she added an ominous understatement: "His voyage has not been so good as we expected." [117] Indeed it had not. Within two weeks Richard had called a meeting of John's creditors at a coffeehouse, apparently to explain John's position and try to gain time. An appeal was also made to John Wordsworth, Sr. to give cash to one creditor, repayable after the sale of John's homeward cargo. At the same time, Richard promised that another creditor's bill of over a thousand pounds would be met as soon as possible.[118]

By the end of the year, however, John had some encouragement. The price of the teas and other goods he had bought in China had risen sharply since September, giving him some two thousand pounds more than he had expected, to offset his losses outbound. And his future prospects had begun to improve in May, when the Bad Earl of Lonsdale died and was succeeded in the viscounty by a distant relation, William Lowther, who set about paying his predecessor's debts as fast as his means would allow. John wrote Dorothy the welcome news that the settlement was to begin at Christmas, and copied at length the accounts which Richard had submitted to Lord Lowther. The first payment on the agreed settlement of £8,500 was actually made on March 1st, following an appeal by Richard to James Graham, Lord Lowther's agent, for three or four thousand pounds for John's investment.[119] The initial installment was three thousand pounds, which was distributed, as Richard's accounts noted, "according to the custom of York"—that is, the four younger children shared nine-tenths of the sum, and Richard, who had already inherited the bulk of his father's estate including his real estate holdings, received the remaining one-tenth.[120]

On February 20, immediate payment of the money had been promised. Almost at once began an agitated correspondence, which threatened to put a severe strain on the Wordsworths' family loyalty. John began it by rashly offering Richard's security for any money that William and Dorothy would lend out of the Lowther payment. Dorothy agreed to lend her share on those terms.[121] On March 26, however, Richard wrote to William: "I cannot engage to make *myself liable to all his* [John's] *creditors* neither is [it] reasonable that I should—you have therefore to say whether you & Dorothy will let him have your shares or not—Christopher has consented." [122] The peremptoriness of Richard's statement was matched by John's next demand: ". . . It is absolutely necessary that I should have the whole of the three thousand pounds." He went on to prove that only three hundred pounds apiece would be an outright, unsecured loan; this was technically accurate in view of his expectations, but to begin by insisting on the whole sum was decidedly tactless. Dorothy remembered his statement and quoted it with emphasis in reply to a letter of Richard's which questioned the justice of her demands on him. If her brothers were willing to lend their shares without security, she was not: she was risking not only her money but her independence. Furthermore, Richard, with his inheritance and his law training, ought to have been willing to underwrite a larger share of the risk than William.[123] Here, apparently, the matter rested. John took Dorothy's share along with her brothers'; however, the withdrawal left no trace in Richard's final accounts, drawn up at the time of his death in 1816, where William's and Dorothy's portion of the initial payment of £3,000 is shown resting undisturbed and drawing annual interest to the date of accounting.[124]

It has been suggested that late in 1802 or early in 1803 came a crisis in John's personal life—that, having been forced to give up Mary Hutchinson, he transferred his affections, or at least his allegiance, to her sister Sara and asked her to become his wife.[125] Of his fondness for Sara the letters leave no doubt. Of any real involvement on his part, however, and certainly of any such definite step as a proposal to Sara, all that can be said is that there is no objective evidence whatsoever. Sara's surviving letters give us no hint of any such matter. William mentioned Sara's part in John's happiness during his 1800 visit; but she shared this role with a list of four others—Dorothy, Coleridge, Mary, and William himself.[126] The fact that John was planning to build himself a house gives no indication who else, if anyone, was to live in it.[127] In fact our only direct information on the subject comes from Coleridge, and Coleridge is hardly a reliable source for anything relating to Sara Hutchinson. Trapped by the Pantisocracy scheme into marriage with an unintelligent, inept, and sometimes fretful wife (who in all justice had reason enough to complain), Coleridge had sought escape from this and his other failures in a hopeless attachment to Sara. Perhaps the hopelessness, which freed him from any new demands for action, was part of its appeal. It was a fantasy-love, a gathering-point for all his unfulfilled aims, and there was always a touch of unreality about it. Once, in a frenzy of tortured apprehension, he persuaded himself that Sara had been in bed with William Wordsworth.[128] His belief, or wish, about John and Sara had no better basis in fact. Indeed, he never stated it except as a wish or a hope. "O dear John Wordsworth!" he wrote in his notebook after John's death. "Ah that I could but have died for you & you have gone home, married S. Hutchinson, & protected my poor little ones." [129] An earlier passage shows even more clearly that he had deliberately imagined the relationship; it was a perverse expression of his love for Sara, enabling him to take satisfaction in his desire for her welfare and at the same time to enjoy tormenting himself with jealousy. ". . . O blessed Sara, you whom in my imagination at one time I so often connected with him [John], by an effort of agonizing Virtue, willing it with cold sweat-drops on my Brow!" [130] On this "effort of agonizing Virtue" the whole story of the intended marriage rests.

Grisedale Tarn, a small mountain lake south of Helvellyn near the summit of the pass between Grasmere and Patterdale. By the foot of the tarn, within sight of Ullswater, William and Dorothy Wordsworth parted from their brother John when he left Grasmere for the last time in September, 1800. (Photograph by C. H. K.)

Wyke Regis Church, near Weymouth, Dorsetshire. John Wordsworth and other victims of the wreck of the *Earl of Abergavenny* are buried in an unmarked grave in the churchyard. (Photograph by C. H. K.)

In short, John's commitments in the spring of 1803 were wholly financial. We do not know the whole amount of his investment. His assets presumably included Lord Lowther's £3,000; £2,000 from Richard; £1500 from Captain Wordsworth Senior; £200 from Robert Griffith; William and Dorothy's £357; £470 from his uncle William Cookson,[131] and £300 which Richard and Christopher borrowed from one of Christopher's acquaintances at Oxford.[132] Some of this, however, may have been offset by debts from the last voyage. On April 21, 1803, Richard drafted a request to Lord Lowther: "Upon the winding up of my Brother's affairs of the last Voyage I am sorry to say they do not look out so favourable as was expected and that the Sum recēēd will not be adequate & sufficient for his purposes. If your Lordship could order the further payment of One Thousand Pounds on acct any time within the course of a Month or six Weeks, such additional payment would make my Brother quite comfortable." He would not have troubled his Lordship, he adds, "if it had not been of very considerable importance to other parts of our Family in so far as they are interested [in] my Brother's welfare." [133] It was July, however, before another payment, this time of £1500, was made.

The *Abergavenny* had started downriver on May 3. Her crew was the usual gang of ruffians and ne'er-do-wells, and on May 30 there was a threat of trouble.

Finding a Spirit of Disaffection to prevail in the Ship it was judged necessary in a Consultation of Commander and sworn Officers, to punish Michael Gretoup with one Dozen Lashes, for Insolence to the Captain & Mr Baggot which was accordingly done. Previous to the Punishment several of the People ran forward in a mutinous Manner, singled out one of the Ringleaders Wm Davies and punished him with 2 Dozen Lashes, also one of the Chinese with one Dozen for attempting to stab with a Knife one of the Boatswains Mates in the Execution of his Duty.

This cool, prompt enforcement of discipline reveals a new side of the normally mild-mannered John in his role as commander.

The *Abergavenny* reached China early in September, a remarkably fast passage of only four months which enabled her to avoid "the violent tufoon" that damaged other ships in the fleet. John's investment sold "neither ill nor well." Despite his early arrival he was detained in China for five months altogether; the peace of Amiens had ended in May, 1803, and the Company authorities in China were waiting anxiously for a warship to protect the fleet or, at least, late news from England brought by the *Woodford*. The *Woodford* took eight months to make the trip, however, and no warship appeared. Since the rest of the fleet was already loaded, it was decided to leave the *Woodford* behind (she appears in official lists with the ships of the next season) [134] and to depend on the heavily armed Indiamen to protect the "country ships" which visited only Asian ports.

The authorities had reason to worry. Near the island of Pulo Aor, about forty miles off the Malayan Peninsula, the French Admiral Linois had been hovering about for several months, waiting for the China fleet to pass by on its way into the Straits of Malacca. With his 74-gun line-of-battle ship Linois had three frigates and a brig. At about 8 A.M. on February 14, he sighted the first of the twenty-eight merchantmen in the enemy fleet. All day long the two forces watched each other, cautious of closing within gunshot. The English Commodore, Dance, sent out five ships to reconnoiter, then drew them back into line. About sunset the French fleet closed the gap, but moved off again without attacking. Dance interposed a line of Indiamen between the country ships and the French, but there was no action during the night.[135] At sunrise, to quote the *Abergavenny*'s log:

> . . . ye Enemy was on ye Weather Beam Dis^{ce} ab^{t} 4 Miles. At 7 ye Com^{e} made ye Sig^{l} to form ye Order of Sailing . . . & ye Enemy made Sail after us, At 10 ye Sig^{l} to close at 11 ye Sig^{l} to prepare for Action. . . . At noon ye Com^{r} . . . hailed & ordered all ye Ships to tack in succession, About this Time ye Enemy began to engage ye Royal George who was headmost Ship.

But Linois had been alarmed from the first by the apparent strength of the opposing fleet. "Twenty of their ships had the appearance of two-deck vessels. We thought we discovered a frigate." Now a shift of wind and the maneuvers of the British placed him in a cross-fire. "There was no longer time to deliberate. . . ."; [136] he broke off his attack and set sail to the northeast. The *Abergavenny*'s log continues:

> Made Sail in chase as did ye Fleet, ye Royal George who being headmost Ship, stood ye Heat of ye Engagement made at 2 PM ye Sig^{l} for Medical Assistance, perceived several Shot Holes in her Sails and Hull; At ½ past 3 ye Com^{r} made ye Sig^{l} to tack, in tacking we fired two Guns at ye Enemy supposing ourselves within Gunshot. . . . At 6 ye Enemy nearly out of Sight steering to ye Northward.

Thus, with two well-intended cannon shots, began and ended the *Abergavenny*'s share in the action off Pulo Aor. Linois was reportedly arrested for cowardice,[137] but his inadequacies in no way dampened the enthusiasm of the British for the victory of their merchantmen. The colony at Malacca saluted the fleet with twenty-one guns. On

August 22, the Directors of the East India Company offered a more practical tribute—cash payments to each of the fleet commanders, with a valuable piece of commemorative silverware, and lesser amounts of cash to the ships' crews. John's share was 500 guineas and a "piece of plate" worth 50 guineas [138]—altogether more than four times his wages for the trip.[139] The brief battle was described by Marryat in *Newton Forster* and made the subject of a painting by Thomas Buttersworth.

The *Abergavenny* had anchored in Northfleet Hope at 3 P.M. on August 14, 1804.[140] John left the ship at once and by the next morning had begun his campaign for a more profitable voyage. The £3,000 that he had already received from Lord Lowther was more than his share of the total settlement of £8500; hence he had gained nothing when the two notes that paid the last of the debt were cashed on July 7.[141] To persuade English tradesmen to extend him credit, and to profit fully from the space allotted him for private trade, John needed a voyage on which China was not the only trading stop. He began immediately calling on or writing to anyone whose influence might possibly help him. Beginning with William Dent, the managing owner of the *Abergavenny,* he then appealed to the Deputy Chairman of the Board of Directors, Charles Grant, Sr.; Thomas Wallace, an Assistant Commissioner of the Board of Control, which superintended the East India Company's activities; Lord Abergavenny, one of the owners of the ship named for him and son-in-law of the powerfully influential John Robinson; and several of the Company's directors or proprietors. He was sick with anxiety half the time, but in mid-September his efforts were rewarded with "a voyage far beyond my expectation, I had almost said my wishes." Sir Francis

Baring had given him, through Mr. Dent (whose approval of course was necessary), the right to choose among the available voyages for the season, after four other captains had made their selections. There were four Bombay and China voyages; John assumed that these would be taken by the first four commanders, leaving him a Bengal voyage. In fact, the Chairman had reserved the Bengal voyage for his protégé Captain Hamilton, and John for a while had a Bombay voyage instead. Hamilton, however, who had not been consulted about the Bengal voyage, turned it down as too risky—it was a new venture—and John, with Dent's approbation, took it over.

Here at last, it seemed, was the opportunity he had been waiting and working for. Retirement, the house in Grasmere, help for William's great work, now were almost within reach. "I shall make a very good voyage of it if not a *very great* one," he wrote to William in January 1805. His investment was about £20,000, which might pay as much as £10,000 on the first leg of the voyage alone; his passengers, who paid their fare by private contract with the captain, must have been worth a minimum of £3,300, probably much more;[142] between Bengal and China he could profit handsomely by rice and the forbidden opium trade and gain still more by teas on his voyage home.

After some delay in taking leave of the Court of Directors,[143] John, with the two servants allowed him by the Company, boarded the *Abergavenny* and sailed for the Downs. Here he had an escape that he called "extraordinary . . . good luck." A heavy gale was blowing in from the westward, and the *Warren Hastings,* dragging her anchor, drifted foul of the *Abergavenny* and crashed into her starboard bow. The *Hastings* was seriously damaged:

"her gun and poop decks are compleately torn up," John wrote; she managed to sail round to Portsmouth with the fleet but then had to be left behind in His Majesty's Yard for repairs. Most fortunately, said John, the damage to the *Abergavenny* was quite minor. Otherwise she too might have been delayed by expensive repairs—and John was determined "to arrive in Bengal the first ship."

From Portsmouth he wrote to William (saying among other things that he liked the *Lyrical Ballads* more than most of his later poems), to his cousin Captain Wordsworth, and a short note of farewell to Christopher: "If I have the good fortune to arrive in England safe I will threaten you with the first visit." On Friday, February 1, the *Abergavenny,* accompanied by four other Indiamen, an escorting frigate, and two whaling vessels, set sail with a fair wind. In the late afternoon John sent back an official letter to the Committee of Shipping: ". . . the Ship Earl of Abergavenny is now under weigh all well."

The fleet sailed between the Isle of Wight and the Needles,[144] a group of chalk pinnacles rising high out of the waters of the Channel. Somehow, in the course of the passage, the Indiamen were separated from their escort, the 44-gun *Weymouth.* They lay to for a time, then tacked slowly westward against a heavy sea and contrary winds, but failed to sight the convoy. Sunday morning found them off Portland. Here the *Abergavenny* was overtaken by a sloop hired by two of her officers and an ensign of the King's troops, who had been left behind when she sailed from Portsmouth.[145]

All through the next day the fleet battled squally westerly winds and a rolling sea; the passengers and soldiers crowded below decks on the *Abergavenny* were miserably sick. By the morning of the 5th she was still only thirty miles west of Portland. Captain Clarke of the *Wexford,* who as senior commander was commodore of the fleet, decided to wait out the weather and give the convoy another chance to appear. He gave signals to bear up, then to sail back into Portland Harbor.[146]

South of the Dorset coast, the rocky Bill of the Isle of Portland extends some four miles out into the Channel. To the east of the Isle, almost at the surface when the waves are rough, lies a boat-shaped bank of rock and stones known as the Shambles, "on account of the number of poor mariners who are annually lost on them," explained Charles Lamb in a manuscript note.[147] The harbor is north of the Isle, between it and the mainland, but approachable only from the east. Tides set powerfully round the Bill, at the rate of six or seven knots, the ebb tide bearing strongly west from eastward of the Shambles. Thus a vessel sailing from the west on the ebb had to steer clear of the Bill and continue well to the east of the Shambles before proceeding north and west toward the harbor.

In the afternoon or evening of February 5, Commodore Clarke reported to the East India Company that his fleet was at anchor in Portland Roads "with the exception of the Earl of Abergavenny." [148] John's ship may have been leading the fleet when the order came to put about, for she was sternmost when the ships returned to Portland.[149] The last to pick up a pilot, she missed the flood tide on which the rest of the fleet made harbor. The ebb was in full force as she turned north to round the eastern end of the Shambles. Aware of the danger, John asked the pilot, "Are you sure you have your marks open?" (that is, have a clear view of the points on shore you are steering by). He replied, "I am." [150] As he spoke, the sails suddenly fluttered, then hung slack: the *Abergavenny* had been caught in one of the unpredictable flat calms that are so common off Portland when the wind changes. Seized by the tide, unsteerable, she was swept toward the white line of breakers that marked the Shambles. A sea drove against her port quarter and stopped her with her head to the north, and she crashed onto the rocks. John's first thought was of his dream of independence, for himself and his family, lost forever with the wealth that was stored in the crushed hull of his ship. He turned with a cry: "O Pilot, you have ruined me!" [151]

Who was at fault? William Wordsworth, who was eager to clear his brother of any kind of blame, laid great stress on John's distrust of pilots, and added, "His own ship was lost while under the management of the Pilot, whether mismanaged by him or not I do not know." [152] The statement is seemingly judicious but the implication is plain. One of the pamphlets issued after the wreck also blamed the pilot; [153] and Thomas Gilpin, the fourth mate, commented acidly, "The Pilot, if he may so be call'd, is saved." [154] Here, experience and firsthand observation must be balanced against professional prejudice and, perhaps, distrust of one not of the ship's crew. The facts, however, seem clear enough. The *Abergavenny* lost her motive power at the most dangerous point of a necessarily dangerous passage. It is hard to see how, under the circumstances, the most competent pilot could have prevented the wreck.[155]

The first shock had come not long after 5 P.M. John immediately set about giving orders; a great deal could still be done to try to save the ship. The carpenter was sent into the hold to report on the condition of the hull. Gun crews began firing signals, but the wind had shifted to the northwest and carried the sound of the cannon away from Portland and Weymouth.[156] In a desperate attempt to push the ship over the Shambles and into open water, John ordered the reefs taken out of her sails and her topsails hoisted to catch the new breeze. But she could not get clear; instead, she was repeatedly lifted off by the cross-surges of the surf, then caught again by the tide and beaten against the rocks.

At first, the carpenter had reported only six inches of water in the hold,[157] but the repeated battering had let in the sea to a depth of several feet. John ordered the King's and Company's troops to the pumps. Working at top speed, they slowed the gradual climb of the water into the hold, then halted it between three and four feet.[158] Outside, the wind was mounting to a gale; but the tide had turned. At half past seven, the *Abergavenny* beat her way clear of the Shambles.

At once John found himself faced with a new set of decisions. He was responsible to his passengers, to the Company for the India dispatches, to the owners and himself for the ship. For the passengers there were two choices. He could try to put them ashore in the ship's boats, which seemed all too likely to be swamped in the heavy swell. This would mean transferring men from the sails and pumps.[159] Or he could run the *Abergavenny* itself ashore at Weymouth, where the gradual slope of the beach meant that no surf would impede rescue operations. But could the *Abergavenny* be kept afloat long enough? The carpenter had been making another inspection. Now he reported grim news: there was a major leak under the chain pumps. He could not repair it, and the water had begun to gain on the pumps.[160] John made up his mind. He ordered the crew to set the jib and foresail,[161] and the helmsman to steer for the nearest shore.

The *Abergavenny* responded heavily, lurching forward

at about three miles an hour[162] with a wind that had shifted to the east. The firing went on, still unheard from the shore; four lights were hoisted at the peak of the mizzenmast. Between eight and nine, the water in the hold had increased to eleven feet; bailing began at the forescuttle and hatchway. It was quite useless. By nine the ship was heavily waterlogged and almost unmanageable. John ordered the steersman to hold the tiller hard astarboard so that the rudder could bite as strongly as possible against the ship's almost imperceptible motion.

About eight o'clock a skiff from a sloop, or according to another account a pilot boat,[163] came alongside and embarked several of the passengers—a Bengal merchant named Evans, his daughter and her companion, another merchant, and a cadet. Mrs. Blair, a widow bound for India to settle her late husband's affairs, refused to risk going in a tiny boat in such a sea.[164] As the Evanses were embarking, John came to the side of the ship and said to them, with emphasis, "God bless you!"[165] It was a typical gesture of kindly concern in the midst of his tormenting responsibilities, and a fair measure of his coolness and efficiency in the crisis. One of the eyewitnesses, Midshipman Benjamin Yates, recalled that he was "quite composed"; Gilpin remembered him as "perfectly corlacted and giving his orders with firmness."[166] His officers were equally collected: one of them stationed himself with a brace of pistols at the door of the spirit room and guarded it against the crew.[167]

But it was all too clear that the chances of beaching the *Abergavenny* were dwindling. John had ordered his crew to cut the lashings of the boats, the spars, anything that a man might cling to and float free of the ship if she went down.[168] Many of those who were saved owed their lives to this piece of forethought. The skiff, or pilot boat, had promised to return for more passengers, but the choppy swell prevented her. It was time to seek more help and to see to the safety of the ship's papers. The *Abergavenny*'s cutter, a small boat ordinarily used for short trips to other vessels of the fleet, was hoisted up and tilted out into the scooping waves. She was manned by half-a-dozen seamen and two officers. One was the purser, C. H. Stewart, who was responsible for the papers. It can hardly have been an accident that the other was John's cousin, third mate Joseph Wordsworth.[169] Someone also saw to it that "some valuable prints which had been sent out for General Lake" went along.[170]

The jib and foresail were kept up, but failed to make the *Abergavenny* respond to her helm. She was settling fast; by half-past ten the water was above her orlop deck.[171] A few minutes later, First Mate Samuel Baggot climbed up from the quarter deck to the poop deck and spoke to his commander. "We have done all we can, Sir; she will sink in a moment." John looked him steadily in the face. "It cannot be helped," he said; "God's will be done." [172] They talked for a short while; then Baggot shouted to the midshipmen to take care of themselves and jumped down on the quarter deck.[173] Cornet Burgoyne, of the 8th Light Dragoons, had fetched up some bottles of cordial from his private liquor supply. He approached the Captain and persuaded him to drink a glass, then another, before handing the rest of the bottle to the seamen near him. This was the beginning of a rumor that John was hopelessly drunk when the ship went down.[174]

At eleven o'clock the *Abergavenny* was a little more than two miles offshore and about twenty minutes from her goal of being grounded on the sand off Weymouth.[175]

Suddenly a gust of wind and an abrupt swell struck her; she was laid almost on her beam ends, then plunged forward to sink head foremost in 66 feet of water.[176] John was standing on the fore part of the poop deck between the mizzen and the starboard ladder leading to the quarter deck. As the wave struck he was repeatedly shouting an order to "haul on board the main tack"—that is, extend the mainsail to the wind by pulling down its lower corners. Baggot and the pilot protested: a sail on the mainmast was useless when the ship had no steerage way. Yates said afterward that he believed the mainsail "hurred her down." He urged the captain to climb into the mizzen rigging, but their voices were lost in a tumult of screaming and confusion.[177] Seaman Webber said he saw the captain climb up on a chicken coop which was kept on the poop deck.[178]

As the bow dipped under, a wave crossed the decks from front to rear in a huge column. It struck Cadet Robert Gramshaw as he tried to climb the stairs to the poop deck, floated him overboard, then washed him up against the mizzen shrouds. He clung on.[179] Gilpin had run to the poop deck and was climbing the shrouds when the sea caught him. He, too, clung on and mounted the ropes as the *Abergavenny* settled to the bottom. She had been listing to port, but she did not capsize.[180] The tops of her masts jutted above the icy water, with a host of survivors hanging from them in the bitter cold of the February night.[181]

The wave had swept Webber overboard with it. He thought he saw it sweep the Captain away also. Midshipman White, floundering in the waves, seized the hencoop, floated on it till it upset, then rode a piece of flotsam to safety in the mizzen rigging.[182] But John had probably climbed from his position just before the wave struck; Gilpin, from high up in the rigging, caught sight of him, among several others, hanging to a rope made fast to the mizzenmast. Clambering down to within ten or twelve feet of him, Gilpin hailed him as loudly as he could and threw him a rope. But John was "Motionless and insensible (it was excessive cold)." "He did not katch the rope or answer," "and was soon after sweep'd away, and I see him no more."[183] Gilpin had done his best. When John was past help, Gilpin carried several others (Cadet Gramshaw among them) up the rigging to safety, and kept their spirits up as well as he could during the long wait for rescue.[184]

Some time after midnight a sloop's boat finally approached and took the survivors from the rigging, twenty at a time. Others had managed to drift to safety on bits of wreckage. In all, of 387 persons aboard, 155 were saved.[185]

A few (my soul oft sees that sight)
Survive upon the tall mast's height;
But one dear remnant of the night—
For Him in vain I seek.

By dawn, the *Abergavenny* had settled another eight feet into a mudbank. Boats now swarmed around her, stripping the valuable rigging from her masts while the cutter *Greyhound* stood guard against looting.[186] Letters describing the wreck were sent to London, where on the following day the officials of the Company began the dreary business of interviewing eyewitnesses, preparing passenger lists, providing funds for survivors. On February 12, a group of 21 crewmen of the *Abergavenny*, who had petitioned for relief, were voted two guineas each as a stopgap if they came to London to collect it. Next day five cadets, the only survivors out of the original twenty-six, were granted a hundred guineas each, to compensate for their losses in baggage and passage money. The same amount was granted the assistant surgeon on February 26. Other officers reentering the Company's service were awarded gratuities on April 5, and the tireless Gilpin, who was among them, got £25 more—officially, to buy a piece of commemorative silver. Rewards were given to the mayor and other officials at Weymouth who had assisted survivors, and to the crews of the rescue ships.[187] Meanwhile the Company had been receiving a stream of offers to contract for the salvage of the *Abergavenny* or her cargo. The job was finally awarded to Messrs. A. and I. Lindegreen or Lindegrens. They apparently did not succeed in raising the ship, however. On August 13 another offer was submitted by Thomas Harrison "in the event of the present Undertaking failing," and more than a year after the wreck the cargo was still being recovered piecemeal—forty-one chests of dollars on May 8, 1806, a number of brass guns and howitzers in October.[188]

The corpses of the drowned floated ashore among the wreckage or were recovered by dragging. John's body was not found until March 20.

> Six weeks beneath the moving sea
> He lay in slumber quietly.[189]

His purser, C. H. Stewart, identified him. A distant relative of Priscilla Wordsworth arranged his funeral, which was "most respectfully attended by twelve Mourners," including the former Mayor of Weymouth.[190] The body was buried in the churchyard at Wyke Regis, in a grave shared by other victims of the wreck. No stone marks the spot; one was originally placed there, but it was recognized by a later Bishop as the top of an old altar table and removed to the sanctuary.[191]

The final official word on the wreck came from the East India Company, among whose concerns was the fact that a charge of negligence would have affected the *Abergavenny's* insurance.[192] On February 13, 1805, the Committee of Shipping was ordered to inquire into the circumstances of the disaster and to report to the Court of Directors. The hearing was held, and the report submitted, on the 19th. On the 26th the Court voted as follows:

RESOLVED UNANIMOUSLY that the Commander, Officers & Ship's Company of the Earl of Abergavenny be fully acquitted of all Imputation of neglect or misconduct in respect to the Loss of that Ship,

That this court are further Unanimously of Opinion that the Earl of Abergavenny was fully & sufficiently found in Anchors, Cables, & other Stores and that the Owners be therefore fully acquitted of all Imputation of neglect or misconduct, in respect to the loss of the said ship.[193]

That should have ended it; but apparently someone questioned the authority of the Court because some of its members were absent. On March 11, 1807, the Directors reconsidered the report from the Committee of Shipping, and again voted unanimously to acquit both officers and owners. This time the resolution records specifically that more than eighteen Directors (out of twenty-four) had voted.[194] Thus the Court, with the official ponderousness that had so often plagued John during his lifetime, gave him, two years after his death, his final vindication.

He had long since been justified in the eyes of his brother and sister. William had set about establishing John's blamelessness with an anxiety which, even allowing for grief and shock, seems to hint at some deep uneasiness within himself. In what ways had John, despite his long absences, provided his brother not only with kinship of feeling but with support and reassurance? The letters, and the comments of those who knew John best, may help provide an answer.

John's most obvious characteristic would, at the very least, have been no barrier between him and the increasingly egocentric William. He was intensely shy—"shy, almost to disease," his brother said. Coleridge's daughter Sara, who thought that the references to John in the memoir of William by his nephew Christopher were "among the most interesting passages it contains," remarked that "his shyness & taciturnity evidenced a something peculiar in his nervous system." [195] We do not know the origins of this shyness, which is less apparent in the rest of the family. It led to the same love of solitude that William turned to such advantage; nothing suited John better than an all-day ramble over the hills with his fishing gear. In his profession, reserve was both a liability and an asset. Probably there was a certain amount of unrecorded misery on his early voyages when he was crowded into the gun-room with the high-spirited midshipmen who were finding their way noisily to a new maturity. But as an officer and particularly as Captain he was expected to keep more or less to himself. The £30 worth of books which he asked William to recommend for his voyage must have been carefully read and re-read, and there were long night watches: "The stars and moon were his chief delight,—he made of them his companions when he was at Sea, and was never tired of those thoughts which the silence of the night fed in him." [196] As to his professional competence, this seems to have been a matter apart from his personality. The man whom his shipmates called "the Philosopher" (*NL* 17) knew when to reef a topsail and when to have an impudent seaman flogged, and did both with promptness and efficiency. All the evidence supports the careful estimate made by Mr. Evans, a passenger, after the wreck:

> In all his conduct, of which I was the witness, I only observed steadiness, judgment and ability, and in the serious hour of danger firmness and resolution, which to the last he manfully maintained.
>
> It may be conceived that the mild and reflecting character of your Brother was not so well calculated for the scenes he had to encounter as others who had less feeling, which imposes the appearance of more energy; but as far as I can judge, he tempered his character with qualities that rendered him equal to the arduous struggles of the profession he had adopted.[197]

It was only in secondary matters, such as dealing with tradesmen or presiding at the Captain's table, that his shyness and inexperience were sometimes a handicap. Admittedly, though, he never fitted the landsman's image of a sailor. "I never heard an oath or even an indelicate expression or allusion from him in my life," William wrote.[198] His habits made him something of an alien even to his fellow captains, whose "*dashing* away in high style on shore" he "could never bear was my fortune ever so large." This was not priggishness, or even stinginess—rather, it was a taste for enjoyments that the bars and streets of Portsmouth and Canton were not equipped to supply.

For John, despite his shyness, was not cold or aloof,

though it took time to know him well. "Our Brother," William wrote, "was so modest and shy a man, that not a tenth part of his worth, above all, his Taste, Genius, and intellectual merits was known to anybody but ourselves and Coleridge." [199] "Ourselves," of course, included Mary, and it was Mary's understanding and responsiveness that called forth John's special regard for her. But he was well enough liked too by those he dealt with merely in the way of business. "I met in the streets four diff[t] people who all gave me very pressing invitations to dinner &c.," he wrote in 1800. "M[r] Dent . . . has also invited me to his house to stay with [him] as often and as long as I like," he said in 1804, at the height of his campaign for a better voyage; and, a few weeks later, "the Chairman [of the Board of Directors] . . . has sent for me several times since I first saw him and offered to send letters overland or to afford me any assistance in that or any other way in his power." John owed a great deal to the influence of his relatives, but something as well to his own personality.[200] Except when he is intent on money matters, his letters seldom fail to reveal natural courtesy and the spontaneous tact which impressed Coleridge. He was a favorite with his young cousins in Norfolk, perhaps because there was a youthful enthusiasm about him, "a gladness which is seldom seen but in very young people," [201] as he pointed out some unnoticed detail in the fields or the gardens at Forncett. Long after his death, Dorothy remembered how his face lighted up when he smiled.[202] As we might expect, he was accommodating ("I like to give people their own way") and concerned for the welfare of others, as his passengers knew. Toward William's powers as a poet he was deferential and self-effacing; William's welfare was his life-work. But his deference, toward William or anyone else, never erased his common sense or his sharp critical eye.

There is, in fact, a carping strain in John that at first may appear surprising. Though William tended to forget it after his death, John's personality had a keen edge; like Dorothy, he could hit hard at the things that displeased him. Quite possibly his shyness dammed up a reserve of suppressed hostility; he may have welcomed an occasional chance to speak his mind about someone, if only in the privacy of his letters. Certainly the list of things he disliked is remarkably long: Penrith, the nobility and gentry, Longman, Gallow Hill, the Court of Directors, "churchiness," his brother Christopher, John Myers, Priscilla Lloyd, and Americans ("a bad race"). His manner of venting his feelings ranged from a forthright blast ("those vile and abominable monsters," "a most damnable Jew") to quiet sarcasm ("[Captain Wordsworth's] Friends Sir W. and Lady Lawson are expected at Bath . . . O the pleasure of being with such great people—"). His underlinings, in particular (indicated here in italic type), are apt to be marks of irony. Occasionally he is his own target. His anxiety at the delay in beginning his 1801 voyage is bearable, he tells Mary, because "I . . . have the pleasing satisfaction of having some of my friends in the same predicament with myself." He makes fun of his exalted rank as Captain ("how great a man I am on board my great ship") and even the style of his own letters: after wandering into a paragraph full of pompous inanities, he pulls himself up short with, *"This you must believe I think very fine."* Like Dorothy, he seems to have escaped the family tendency to take oneself too seriously.

John was, in short, a modest, likable man, tactful, sometimes sentimental, with quietly shrewd insight and a dry wit salted with irony. His death was understandably hard to bear. It was a singularly bitter blow to William, who had learned to depend on his brother as an unfailing source of support for his own values.

Before John's shipwreck, William, in "Resolution and Independence" and the "Ode to Duty," had begun to praise a stoicism that he himself did not yet possess. ("He wrote his Ode to Duty," said a friend, "and then he had done with that matter.") He had, almost without exception, lived as he pleased, "as if life's business were a summer mood." True, what pleased him, in his more secure moments, was poetry; he worked hard enough at a calling which seemed to need no vindication. But "Resolution and Independence" contains vivid proof that his confidence was profoundly undercut by doubt. From the time of his uncles' displeasure at his idleness in the 1790s he must have asked himself often what right he had to shirk the world's duties. Part of his admiration for John, then, may have been based on the great difference in their lives. For John had chosen a profession which meant loneliness, isolation, discomfort, bodily stress, and the ever-present danger of death. A glance at any contemporary newspaper will show how constant was the risk of shipwreck. John's letters speak of long nights of exposure to cold and sleet, a collision in a gale, a naval battle with the French. He could not have performed even the barest essentials of his duty without justifying William's praise of him as "brave," "resolute," "manly." John was acting out in hard daily experience a role which his brother admired and avoided.[203]

Furthermore, he was undergoing these hardships on William's behalf. It was understood from the beginning that the fortune John hoped to make at sea was to be a family fortune: "I will work for you," he had said. "Could I but see you with a green field of your own and a Cow and two or three other little comforts I should be happy." [204] It was a touching display of affection and loyalty, but it was also an endorsement of William's values, a guarantee that the poet has the right to ask "that others should / Build for him, sow for him, and at his call / Love him." [205]

John's practical support was the more meaningful because it came from a man who intimately understood and valued William's love of poetry and natural beauty. The ties among all the Wordsworth children were strong while they were growing up without parents or a home, and at one time William and Christopher shared a common interest in poetry,[206] but Richard and Christopher had grown away from any special intimacy with the others. Only William, John, and Dorothy shared a close kinship of feeling. John, Dorothy wrote, "would walk with William or me, or both of us, and was continually pointing out . . . something which perhaps would have escaped our observation, for he had so fine an eye that no distinction was unnoticed by him, and so tender a feeling that he never noticed any thing in vain." The more is the pity that he remained "a *silent* Poet." [207] His letters are his only writing that has survived, and in them, with one exception, he attempts neither poetry nor poetic description. The exception is in Letter 25, in a passage which William used as the basis for one of his elegies on John's death.

I have been on shore this afternoon to strech my legs upon the Isle of White. . . .The daisy's after sunset are like little *white* stars upon the dark green fields. . . .The rich wodds & fine bay, the intrest that one must always feel from the ships &

Life there is upon water—the noise of seamen in the evening heard at a distance the boat men & fishermen near the shore—

At first sight this hardly seems to bear out William's, Dorothy's, and Coleridge's praise of John's power of observation. Certainly his expression is anything but poetic; it is the trite, stumbling diction of a man unaccustomed to writing imaginatively. If we disregard the adjectives, however, we see that John has done much more than list at random the pretty or "interesting" things he has seen. The contrasting details blend and fuse to give a sense of unity independent of any logical organization. The passage is, in its unpretentious way, a fair illustration of what Coleridge said the Imagination could achieve in literature. That it stands alone in John's letters proves chiefly that poetry is not what John thought letters were for. As far as can be judged from this one example, William was not merely indulging in self-projection when he believed that John shared his gift of poetic vision. He undoubtedly emphasized this quality in his brother because it offered proof that a practical man, a worker, might still hold William's own values supreme; but his emphasis was not without a basis in fact.

John's comments on William's poems establish yet another link between the two brothers. John loved poetry, though he had little interest in explaining his responses to it.[208] It was his companion on his long voyages, and he found time in the course of his busy days ashore to read and reread his brother's verse, aware that such poems as "Michael" deserved careful re-exploring. He asked William to tell him "what Poets and what Poems he thinks *I would like* most" out of Anderson's collection, "& also . . . which are the best poems": clearly he wanted to develop his taste with William's expert help. (It would be interesting to know whether John's reverent or irreverent side was uppermost when he recorded gravely that "W^{m} says that the nutting and Joanna shew the greatest genious of any poems in the 2^{d} Vol.") On the whole, his selection of favorites among his brother's work does him credit, though we may question his preference for "To the Small Celandine" or "The Mad Mother," or regret that he could read "Tintern Abbey" only once and Coleridge's "The Ancient Mariner" not at all (William had his reservations about it too). A number of his choices have been endorsed by later critics: "Ruth," "The Cuckoo," "Resolution and Independence," "The Thorn," and, of course, *The Prelude*. He seems to have shared with William an interest in the actual as subject-matter; he objects to "The Danish Boy" as "a *wild* story and dream of Fancy" (but he does like the beginning of *Peter Bell*). Though he is warm in his praise, he is by no means uncritical. In 1805 he tells William frankly that some of his latest poems are harsh, and that all of them are inferior to the *Lyrical Ballads*. There is no evidence as to whether or not he followed William in his moments of highest vision, but, as far as his brief comments reveal, he fully understood the spirit and intention of his brother's poetry.

The two men must have found much in common, also, in their views on politics and religion. They both disapproved of Pitt, who William felt put his ambition somewhat ahead of his love of country; [209] John, though he saw a risk in dismissing Pitt in 1801 unless peace followed, wished "they had turn'd him out about 5 or 6 years since" (perhaps around the time of the anti-sedition laws). William would heartily have seconded John's observation, apropos of Coleridge's "marks of humiliation" in his public letter to Fox, that "independence is the order of the day—and a very good order too." William looked with dread at the disappearance of "the spirit of independence," "the blessings of independent domestic life" and of the small landowner before the encroachments of factories and workhouses.[210] John regretted the corruption of the Portsmouth boatmen, poor men who naturally seized their chances to extort money from outbound passengers. "I only hope & trust that in the North of England you will never have a set of men supported by visitors to the Lakes —they will be the very ruin & the hearts ruin of the country." With John's concern for the independent poor, however, went a contempt for the rich and "great" which William seems never to have shared. It would be interesting to know its source: it is bitter and persistent enough to have originated in some personal slight or in some irrational focusing of a shy man's sense of grievance.

As to religion, apart from a conventional "God love thee" now and then, John might have been raised a pagan for all the letters tell us. He mentions the Church only to attack the "churchiness" of his uncle. Other records show him as, at the least, indifferent to his early religious training. As Captain he was expected to perform divine service on Sundays, but, as one of his logs reveals, he often decided that the work of the ship was more important. It is true that he "greatly valued . . . religious instruction for youth," [211] but this was apparently because such training made good sailors by teaching obedience. And his final resignation to "God's will" on the deck of the sinking *Abergavenny* cannot be interpreted as much more than an instinctive reversion to a set of teachings which he had never troubled to rebel against. His creed, what there was of it, was certainly held loosely and easily enough not to conflict seriously with William's trust in the linking of man and nature by benevolent universal being. It is doubtful that John refined his own views of Nature to the extent that William did, or that he consciously looked to Nature for any of the ultimate answers which the apparent void in his religious tenets left unsupplied. But, like Dorothy, he loved Nature in all its subtleties, and this was practical support enough for William's more sophisticated belief. John's long visit to Grasmere in 1800, like Dorothy's influence since 1794, helped to confirm William's profoundly needed faith in Nature and Imagination as sources of truth.

These were the reasons that John's death cut so deeply into William's heart. Taking them all together, there seems little cause to think that William overpraised John greatly in the days after the tragedy. What he seems to have done, rather, was to isolate (and to that extent, admittedly, to distort) the best of John's good traits, particularly those in which he found personal comfort and support—traits which John's shyness, silence, lack of formal training had kept hidden from all but the loving penetration of those nearest to him.

There has, understandably, been much speculation about the permanent effects of John's death on William's life and thought. The force of the blow, the sudden and overwhelming impact of the tragedy, is one of the best-documented facts in William's career; we have seen how the letters of 1805 dwell on his grief.[212] Moreover, the loss of John coincided approximately with what is often viewed as a period of marked changes in William: an early aging process, the passing of his highest imaginative powers, a drift in the direction of religious orthodoxy. William himself, in an often-quoted letter to Sir George Beaumont, suggested that the tragedy had sent him stumbling in the direction of a conventional belief in immortality: "Would it [not] be blasphemy to say that upon the supposition of the thinking principle being destroyed by death, however inferior we may be to the great Cause and ruler of things, we have *more of love* in our Nature than he has? The thought is monstrous; and yet how to get rid of it except upon the supposition of *another* and a *better world* I do not see." [213]

The temptations for conjecture are obvious; but to yield to them would take us far beyond the scope of the present study. We would need to establish, for instance, when William's swing toward orthodoxy began, and how far it went (note that none of the elegies written in John's memory support the idea of an afterlife suggested in the Beaumont letter); to reopen the question of William's poetic decline and its dates; and finally to disentangle John's death from all the possible causes of William's changing tendencies. It is a worthy challenge, but the task is too intricate to be attempted here. Our investigation must be limited to establishing the facts of the relationship between John and his family.

Of this relationship little more remains to be told. The crushing agony which had overwhelmed William and Dorothy with the news of the shipwreck ebbed away gradually as the months passed. William, after a futile first attempt which he was too shaken to record, wrote out his grief in a series of short lyrics: "Elegiac Verses in Memory of my Brother," composed at the spot near Grisedale Tarn where he had parted from John in 1800; "To the Daisy," based partly on John's description of the Isle of Wight (Letter 25); and "Distressful Gift!" which seems to commemorate the transcribing of the other two poems into a book originally meant to accompany John on his voyages. To pay tribute to his brother in the tradition of his craft, and even to record the finality of the event, comforted William; the references to his loss disappear from the letters as 1805 draws to a close. The analysis of John's character that found its way into "The Happy Warrior" at year's end was concise and dispassionate. By the spring of 1806, William found himself able to look steadfastly at Sir George Beaumont's painting of a storm at sea, and to reshape what he saw into the finest of his elegies for John, "Suggested by a Picture of Peele Castle." Here, in a hymn to endurance, Wordsworth's luminous imagery wrought out the final meaning of John's death—the exquisite balance of human experience, in which a light too lovely to be real, a treasure-house reflected in a sea, stand counterpoised with fear, trampling waves, a hulk laboring in a deadly swell.[214]

It was a fitting end to the works of praise and mourning. John had dedicated his welfare and his years of hardship to the support of William's genius, and had sustained William's self-trust with the full loyalty of his gentle and perceptive heart. His death, the abrupt ending of his hopes, had seemed cruel and meaningless. But it was the stimulus of remembered grief that illuminated William's vision as he wrote one of the last of his great poems. "Peele Castle" is such a moment of awareness as Wordsworth had often created from his memories, merging recollected desolation and fear into the image of a world whose sun and storm are the diverse "types and symbols of eternity." Into this renewed insight his feeling of unending loss now blended and was transformed. John, the brave, shy, devoted brother, had touched William's life for the last time. His unforeseen legacy was a gift of pain transmuted into a poet's sober dream, an hour of seeing and, perhaps, some part of the strength underlying many future decades of patient craftsmanship—the harvest of an eye made quiet by its watch over man's mortality.

A NOTE ON THE LETTERS

The text of the letters that follow, which was initially prepared from Xeroxes supplied by Cornell University Library, is based, with three exceptions, on examination of the original manuscripts in the Wordsworth Library at Grasmere. The exceptions are Letter 2, which is in a collection of Wordsworth family papers not kept in Grasmere; Letter 36, which is a quotation in a letter from Coleridge to Thomas Wedgwood; and Letter 51, which is kept in one of John Wordsworth's ledgers in the India Office Library.

The original text of the letters has been reproduced as exactly as possible, except that (1) words deleted by John Wordsworth have been omitted when his correction of them involved no change in meaning; (2) accidental repetitions have been omitted; (3) words which John Wordsworth interlineated to correct obvious mistakes have been placed in normal position without special marking; (4) interlineated words that add to or otherwise change his initial meaning have been placed between carets at the points where he inserted them; (5) in the interest of easier reading, complete sentences have been separated from each other by a long space (John Wordsworth seldom used periods; if he divided two sentences at all, it was usually with a dash).

Cancelled passages and illegible postmarks are in ⟨angle brackets⟩. Readings of these cancellations are necessarily somewhat uncertain but have been inserted whenever possible; illegible passages are indicated by ellipses, and wholly illegible cancellations by empty brackets. Words destroyed where the paper has been torn are shown by {braces}, and conjectural readings inserted whenever possible. John Wordsworth's frequent underscorings have been indicated by italics. The heading "Postmark" includes, for letters mailed outside London, the stamp of the point of mailing, separated by a semicolon from the (circular) mark which shows the date of receipt in London; this mark consists of a letter identifying the postal clerk, followed by the abbreviated month, the day and year. The letters mailed in London all bear an evening postmark; those mailed elsewhere bear a London morning-duty mark.

Routine annotations on the letters, dealing mostly with content (apparently by Christopher Wordsworth, Jr., John's nephew) and date (by Gordon Graham Wordsworth) have not been reproduced; a few unusual entries by other hands are mentioned in the notes.

THE LETTERS

1. To Richard Wordsworth

Address: Mr Richd Wordsworth / A. Parkins Esqr [1] / Grays Inn / London

Postmark: PENRITH; A JY 27 [17]92

Penrith June [for July] 24th 1792 [2]

My dear Brother,

I am much obliged to you for the three guineas you were so kind as to send me; and which arrived safe in due time— I have now another request to make which is that you will [be] good enough as soon as you can make it convenient to send me a Copy of the Note of acceptance which Captn Wordsworth [3] gave you, prior to my going out to India last voyage [4] also what money you paid for my outfit etc. The reason that I want to know all this is—that I am going to Wthaven tomorrow & knowing that C. Words has made a mistake of 10 pound in my account I would wish to settle the matter with him—

Kitt [5] desires his Love to you he intends to go next week to Hawkshead and from thence to Mr Smith att Broughton: [6] where after staying a few days at Wthaven I mean to meet—& we go together to Mr Barkers [7] I intend to set him back again to Hawkshd and shall come over the Fells to Wthaven—

I am Dear Richd Yours sincerely
& Affectionately
JOHN WORDSWORTH

2. To Christopher Crackanthorpe [1]

Address: None (draft)
Postmark: None
Source: WP

[Gravesend,] April 26th 1793—

My dear Uncle,

I am extremely obliged to you, for your kind Letter, which I received only Yesterday owing to my being on board of Ship— [2]

I have another request to ask which is that you would be so kind as let me have that hundred pound of my sisters which is in the Carlisle Bank [3] My Brother Rich'd will give her a bond or any security that may be thought necessary—

I hope you'll excuse my importunity when you consider the situation I am now in; my wages in the ship will be by no means adequate to the expences which must necessarily accrue on the Voyage.[4] The India Company allow all the Officers the privilege of Trade which in my case is intirely done away by the want of money—

On Tuesday night the Sailors belonging to all the Indiamen at Gravesend were impressed by three Frigates sent from Shereness on purpo{se} which has left us in very great distress & will undoubtedly detain us in England much longer that [*for* than] was expected, all the Ships and [*for* had] protections granted them by the Lords of the Admiralty— [5]

I am very glad to hear such a good acc^t of my Cousins that they are both very well—

Brothers join with me in best Love to You my Aunt & Miss Cust [6] & I am

Dear Uncle Yours
Sincerely
JOHN WORDSWORTH
Earl of Abergavenny
Gravesend

[Several practice signatures]

3. To Mary Hutchinson

Address: Miss Hutchinson / Gallow Hill [1] / Wykeham / Near Malton / by York
Postmark: None

[Greta Bridge and Boroughbridge, October 4, 1800]

I am very sorry my dear Mary to be obliged to pass thro' York without having an opportunity of seeing thee at Gallow hill— I had once some thoughts of stopping at York ⟨& then I should certainly⟩ but it is now too late You will have seen by the papers that the Aberga'ny is arrived and I have the pleasure to inform you that Captn Wordsw[orth] [2] has made a very good voyage I do not know whether he goes again or not but I rather think he will for the expences of living are now so great that what might have contented him four or five years ago will now be insufficient When you write to your Aunt Monkhouse [3] you must tell her that my stay in Penrith was so short that it was out of my power to call upon her. I should have liked much to have seen Joanna.[4] the day after I arrived at ⟨Penrith⟩ ^Newbiggin [5]^ I went with Mrs Crackanthorp to Penrith for I wanted to see Mr Parkin his [*for* he] is an owner of the Abergany [6]

I met in the streets four diff^{t} people ⟨in the street & I met Mr Gra⟩ who all gave me very pressing invitations to dinner &c. I did not so much as call at any of their houses for I had not time therefore I thought it was the best to call no where—

Greata Bridge

When I shall see thee again My dear Mary God only knows but that it may be as soon as the nature of my profession will admit of will be the constant prayer of Thine Affectionately

John Wordsworth

Give my best & kindest love to Sara [7] & tell her that I am sorry I had not the pleasure of seeing her at Grasmere this ⟨last⟩ summer & you must also remember me in the kindest manner to Tom & all your Brother[s]

I shall send the Lyrical Ballads down to you when they come out ‸which‸ & ⟨hop⟩ ‸I hope will be soon‸ if I can find a good ⟨opportunity⟩ conveyance & shall then write you a long Account of my proceding in London &c—God bless you Farewell

J. W

Borrough Bridge—Octr 4th

I find the mail does not go nearer to York than Borrough Bridge [8] I hope you will be able to read what I have written I have been much hurried—

4. To Dorothy Wordsworth

Address: Miss Wordsworth / Ambleside / Kendal / W^t^moreland / Single [1]
Postmarks: L^G^ STRATTON; G NOV 13 [1800]

Forncett [2] Novr 10th Monday [1800]

My dear Sister,

You will be surprized to hear that I have been at forncett a week I should have written to you upon my arrival here but I wish'd ^first^ to see W^m^ & Christopher. I went on saturday to the schools which they are at it is ab^t^ 12 miles from Forncett in a very pleasant situation for Norfolk— Christopher I think will be very much like his father he has a high forehead short nose, talks little & is very pale— the other children have all a fine colour in their faces and [are] like each other though not at all in my opinion like their father or mother— Elizabeth the youngest ⟨is very like⟩ ⟨what⟩ ^puts me very much in mind of^ Mary ⟨was⟩ when I was last at forncett [3] they are without exception the finest set of children I ever saw— I should not have known Mary her face is very different to what is [*for* it] was when a child— she is not very handsome [4] but has a much better face than any of the Crackanthorp family— [5]

George talks incessantly—& is very like W^m^ they say Mary is like you as for my part I do not see the smallest resemblance— The house is excellent the garden enlarged, thrown more open and *now* under great improvement— the country at this time looks naked and poor & as I am no sportsman it is a very uninteresting place to be at this time of the year—except for the children with whom I have been much delighted they are much finer children than I ever expected to have found them—

Rich[d] sent me your Letter down & I have written to him to desire that M[r] Wedgewood may be paid immediately—[6] I can do without the 100£ but it is an object to me to get as much money as possible I shall then get my investment upon better term{s} Capt[n] W. is let[ting] me have 2000£ & Rich[d] 2000£ & I have had an offer of 1500£ from a quarter that I did not expect none of our relations or any body that you are acquainted with—

Is the preface to the L. B. to receive any alteration[7] I wish you would let me known as soon as the last poems is sent off that I may be upon the lookout for the vol[s] I have to purchase a number of Copys I am also very impatient to see them as I think [it] is a very great pity that so much time should be lost—

I am glad to hear that you are likely to have Sara H. with you so soon[8] ⟨&⟩ for such a long time— I think Penrith is the most scandalous place I was ever in—every thing one says and does is known to the whole town I am sorry to hear of Jack Hutchinsons intended marriage[9] if he should have any children which I suppose is not impossible I am afraid in these dear times he will have but a bad bargain— I am glad that the Lyoyds[10] have been such good neighbours— Remember me to Coleridge & the Simpsons[11] & to old Molly—[12] & to the Clarksons[13] when you go to Penrith— give my kind love to Mary & Sara Hutchinson—& tell Sara that [I] am sorry that she did not *come sooner to* Grasmere I am to leave forncett on Friday so when you write you will have the goodness to direct to Staple Inn[14] as before— Kitt had left Forncett ab[t] a fortnight before I came here but I hope I shall see him in Cambridge—

I hope I shall be here again befor the ship sails— the Borroughs & all Forncett people have inquired very particularly after you. I was yesterday at a Christening of two of *Mrs Walfords Children.* *Miss D. B* [15]

My Uncle & Aunt desire their kind Love & Mary who say[s] she remembers you perfectly well with yours

Aff^ly J. Wordsworth

I am glad W^m has got so well on with his last poem—[16] Mary had not the smallest recolection of me

The ⟨ ⟩ [17]

5. To Dorothy Wordsworth

Address: Miss Wordsworth
Postmark: None

[11 Staple Inn, November 17, 1800]

My dear Sister,

I rec^d your Letter this morning informing me of the 80£ [1] which had before come safe to Rich^d when I was at Forncett— Wedgewoods money has been paid—& as it is of consequence to me to get as much ready {mone}y as possible I shall be much obliged to you for the 80£—

I am sorry to hear that W^m has been poorly since Stoddart left you.[2] Give my love to him

& I am Yours Aff^ly
John Wordsworth

17th Nov^r

6. To Mary Hutchinson

Address: Miss Hutchinson / ⟨Wykeham / Malton / by York⟩ *Readdressed, in another hand:* Mr J. Hutchinsons / Stockton [1]
Postmark: A DE 5 [1]800

[11 Staple Inn] Decr 5th 1800

My dear Mary,

I received a Letter from my sister a few day[s] ago ^*which was ⟨ten⟩ eleven days upon the road*^ desiring I would endeavour to procure a situation as 4th or 5th mate in our service for your Brother Henry [2] who I am very sorry to learn is out of employment— every apointment in the regular service is now fill'd up and it is neither in my power or in the power of any of my friends to get him into the Service ⟨for⟩ this season many of the ships are now upon the point of sailing. & our fleet which will be the last of season is to sail from the Downs the 7th of March— I can assure you my dear Mary it would have given me the greatest pleasure if I could have afforded him any assistance the officers that were in the Abergavenny last voyage go in her again except the chief mate & that place is now promis'd to a young man—

there are so many young men out of employment in our Service—yet belonging to the Service that I dare say there has been at least 50 applications for the chief Mates berth in the Abergavenny—& by men that have not the smallest chance of getting out this season— our Service is the very worst in the world without a young man has a certainty of getting a command— as for my part I consider myself *as most most* fortunate. & I am sure you will be delighted to hear that in a few weeks I am to be sworn into the command of the Abergavenny Captn Wordsworth has made a very handsome fortune & is going to reside at W^t^haven—*and they* tell *me in 8 or ten* years I *am to* be a very *rich man* for in that time I am to make four voyages— perhaps my sister will have informed you that I have been staying with my Uncle W^m^ in Norfolk— I was exceedingly pleased with the children I think without partiality I never [saw] six finer children in my life— I could only stay a fortnight but in that time I believe I became a great favourite with them George the youngest Boy when I was walking with him in the garden the morning before I came away got a rope & with the assistance of his little sisters would tie me to a tree & said that I should not go away so soon— I do not think any of them are like there father or mother Christopher & W^m^ the two eldest boys are at school— Sara is now at Grasmere & I wish I was ⟨with⟩ there to— O those vile Lyrical Ballads why do they not come out

I think it is a great pity that W^m^ should be loosing so much time [3] I understand ⟨they⟩ from Longman [4] & Arch [5] they could have sold numbers even of the first vol. if it had been publish'd—

I hav{e some} thoughts of going to Cambridge to see Christr [6] I had {the p}romise of a letter from him when I {was} in No{rfolk} but it has not yet appear'd—

Tell me if you want any thing in London before I send you down the L. B. (for they *must come out* before we sail)—& it shall come down with them & I hope you will write to me immediately for nothing will give me greater pleasure than to hear from & of ⟨ ⟩ [7] you & if I could have been of any assistance to your Brother I am sure you will think it unnecessary for me to repeat that nothing would have pleased me so much & I beg you will remember me to him & tell him so—& with my love to y^r Brother Tom

I am My dear Mary Yours ever Affectionately

JOHN WORDSWORTH

Direct to me Mr John Wordsworth N° 11 Staple Inn

7. To Mary Hutchinson

Address: Miss Mary Hutchinson / Mr John Hutchinsons / Stockton upon Tees / Durham
Postmark: A DE 12 [1]800

[11 Staple Inn, December 12, 1800]

My dear Mary,

I rec^d a Letter from my Sister a few days ago requesting that I would endeavour to get an appointment ^as^ ⟨of⟩ 4th or 5th mate in our service for your Brother Henry I wrote to you ^at Gallow Hill^ almost immediately upon the receipt of my sisters letter which ⟨I am sorry to say⟩ was eleven days upon the road to say that it was not in my power to get such an appointment for him— Since that time I have heard that you are at Stockton & am afraid that you have not rec^d my other letter. If I had known sooner I could have got him a place as either 2. 3 or 4 [mate] of one [of] the Tea ships going out to India & commanded by a shipmate of mine & a particular friend but [it] is now too late as the ship is on point of sailing, neither ⟨did⟩ ^could^ I know whether he would like such a situation—

as for our service it is so difficult ⟨every⟩ ^at the conclusion of each^ voyage to get another appointment that I have known young men remain out of employment for three or four years & it is a service I would not recomend to any man— as for my part I consider myself as fortunate in the greatest extreme—

I Congratulate you my dear Mary upon your Brothers Marriage & I beg you will give my Kind Love & Congratulations to him & his Wife— ⟨Ihwas⟩ I am glad that you are at Stockton for I think you must almost be tired of the confinement & want of company at Gallowhill I have discover'd that much retirement is not good for one the great misfortune is that we are all in ⟨the⟩ extremes—

I have been several times to the play since I came to London— the houses are so large that you can hear nothing & I think we shall never see another play well acted upon the London stage—[1] the favorite Pizarro[2] is beatiful in the scenery but the noise rant and flare acting is ^excessively^ disgusting ⟨in the extreme⟩ Shakespears plays are not liked by the town the reason I conceive to be is that many of the beatiful passages are not heard ^& understood^ the houses being so large and I think ^too^ a great deal must be lost in the acting the characters being ^many of them^ more of imagination than reality— I have seen Mr Lewis' Tales of Wonder[3] very poor & Mrs Robinsons L. Tales[4] the same I have got the farmers boy[5] it is not a poem I like much. Colridges Walestein[6] is spoken very lightly of in the month[l]y review—

I am very sorry that the L. Ballads are not forthcoming it is a great pity— W^{m} is loosing time—

I understand Sara is very much pleased with Grasmere I wish I was with them & I might as well be there as here for any good I am doing ⟨here⟩ at the present—only I must not be out of the way. how did you leave Tom & how does he like his farm? I am glad to hear that George has got a farm [7] & I wish Sara & him success ⟨ ⟩ [8] & every ⟨other⟩ good wish that can attend them ⟨ ⟩ [9]— *you see I am like most great men* write ⟨& wr⟩ ‸a‸ very bad and careless hand but I hope you will excuse it

Do let me hear from you immediatly & direct to Mr J. Wordsworth N° 11 Staple Inn & let me know how Harry is going to dispose of himself God bless you my dear Mary & believe me to be

Yours Affectionately. JOHN WORDSWORTH

[*At beginning of letter, upside down:*]

I'll send you the farmers boy Mrs Robinsons L. Tales & the L. Ballads Together (Mr Lewis' Wonderful Tales are in the first place too expensive & the 2^{d} not worth carriage) and any thing else you like—that is any thing you wish

8. To Mary Hutchinson

Address: Miss Hutchinson / Wykeham / Malton / by York

Postmark: ⟨ ⟩JA⟨ ⟩

[11 Staple Inn,] Saturday the 10th of Jan 1801

My dear Mary,

I have the pleasure to inform you that I was sworn into the Command of the Aberga'ny on Wednesday last [1] we are to be in the Downs on the 7th of March & I hope we shall leave Portsmouth before the latter end of March — I have come into a great deal of Business all at once & am now very much hurried— I can assure you I felt very strange & it will take some time ⟨ ⟩ [2] before I shall feel easy under my new acquired title—

the Ship is a very *noble ship* & I have every prospect of

doing well & of being comfortable   indeed I do not know a man so lucky as myself—   Our Service taking it in general is most abominable & detestable

I am sorry My dear Mary that it is not in my power ⟨to service⟩ ^to be of any service to^ your Brother Harry   I am certain he would have liked the appointment which I could have got him had not my Sisters letter come too late—   the ship was an Indiaman tho' not now in the regular Service   she carried 26 Guns & 80 Men—

I was with Mr Stoddart the other morning who read me a long *long essay upon Taste* of his own composition   I was glad to hear from him that Coleridge was to be in town on the 17th of this month   indeed I shall be most happy to see him—   the L. B. are not yet arrived in town [3]   I am very impatient to see them & will send them to you as soon as they ⟨arrive in to⟩ are publish'd with a long history of my proceedings in London—

My Brother Christopher has been staying with us for this last week & left us this morning to go back again to Cambridge   I saw very little of him being myself so much engaged—   he speaks very highly of Mr Loyd & very fairly of Charles so much so that I doubt not but Wm & D. will find them comfortable neighbours—[4]

I suppose George is very impatient to get upon his farm   I am glad to hear from my sister that it is ⟨   ⟩ [5] a good one & that he has it upon good terms.   I make no doubt by this time that you are same *moord* at Gallow Hill Remember me to your Brother Tom & believe me to be

Yours ever affly

JOHN WORDSWORTH

9. To William Wordsworth

Address: M[r] Wordsworth / M[r] Clarkson's / near Penrith / Cumb[d] / to be forward'd to Grasmere if M[r] W. be not at Penrith

Postmark: A JA ⟨3⟩0 [1]801 [1]

[11 Staple Inn, January 30, 1801]

My dear W[m]

I have deliver'd your letters [2] to M[r] Longman who has since told me that they will *all* be *faithfully* sent *to the great men & women* I was much pleas'd with your Letter to M[r] Fox [3] & with the others of course in a smaller degree indeed I should have been very much disapointed if I had not seen them— now I do request that if they answer these letters you will have the goodness to ⟨send⟩ let me know what they say— I cannot express how much everyone that I have seen appears to be delighted with some *one* of your poems & more particularly the Brothers— I have seen Stoddarts review but I thoug[h]t it too flattering I mean too much of a panegyric they will see imediately that it has been written by a friend—& it is to be submitted to the perusal of the *Reviewers* Pinny [4] was much delighted with the Brothers & with the Song [5] the rest he seem'd to think lightly of— John Myers [6] was very ⟨deeply⟩ much indeed affected by the Brothers

& some of my friends that you are not acquainted with have spoke in the *most most* high terms of your poems—[7]

Longman who by the by is a most damnable Jew could not help ⟨showing the⟩ expressing how high M[r] W. character stood in the poetical department & show'd by his looks that he expected to gain a great deal by the Book—

You must tell Sara H. ^with my kind Love^ that I rec[d]

her ⟨kind⟩ letter & good wishes & thank her most kindly for them. Your Poems are sent down & I shall take care that Mary H— go off tomorrow by the Coach— Captn & Mrs W are at Bath I have sent them a Copy—

I have been exceedingly pleased with the poem of the C.[umberland] beggar. I was at the first reading disapointed with Michael at the second reading I was a ⟨little⟩ ^not a little^ pleased—but latterly I have been excessively delighted with it. when I first read it I though[t] the circumstances too minute & the language to low for a blank verse poems ⟨but⟩ from what Stoddart had told me I thought it would have been a poem in rhyme but I now think it more intersting and particularly to those who are acquainted & have lived in Cumbd— Tobin [8] is going to send you Bertrams travels [9] I think Stoddart a very poor judge of Poetry I recd a letter to day from Captn Wordsworth who is much delig[h]ted with Bath—

Mr & Mrs Cook often inquire very kindly after you & have ⟨whish⟩ *desired me several times—to say so.* As for my own business I am coming on most famously I shall soon be as rich *as a Jew*— my investment to China will amount to about 10,000£ & the longer the war last the better it will be for me— thats some comfort. I hope Colridge is better [10] tell him I shall write to him sometime soon I shall if possible send Mr Simpson some Bamboo he may find employment in making the fishing rod which I have sent him into some decent shape

I have written this letter at different times and in great haste so you must excuse mistakes

Remember me to the Clarksons Mr Myers [11] and everyone that asks after me & ⟨I am⟩ With Kind Love to Dorothy I am Your Afft

Brother John Wordsworth

10. To Mary Hutchinson

Address: {   } by Yo{rk}
Postmark: Illegible

[11 Staple Inn, January 31, 1801]

I beg thee ten thousand pardons my Dear Mary for not sending the L. B down as soon as they were publish'd they have (⟨to . . .⟩ [1] been out now about 5 days) [2] but I have been so employ'd & teased that I am sure your *kindness* will excuse me for not proforming my promises ^as soon as I might^—⟨They⟩ ^it^ shall come off this evening by the coach but I send you *this* to apprize you of its coming & I will not pay the carriage for this reason because I think you will be more likely to get the box—The coach which I shall send them by goes to the same Inn as the Scarboro Coach—& you must write immediately to let me know whether you get them or not— Excuse this short note & believe [me] to be (in great haste)

Yours ever Aff^{ly}
John Wordsworth

Staple Inn Jany 31st

11. To Mary Hutchinson

Address: Miss Hutchinson
Postmark: None

[11 Staple Inn, January 31, 1801]

My dear Mary,

I wrote to you this evening a short note by the post [1] telling you that I ⟨had⟩ ^intended^ sending the L. B. down this evening by a coach that goes off later than the mail

& I hope you will receive them safe— I receiv'd a letter from Sara the other day enclosing me a packet of letters from W^{m} to Mr Fox &c. which are now all deliver'd I was much entertain'd with the reading of them I could not help thinking that W^{m} was becoming a most accomplish'd Courtier— Sara is going back to Grasmere when they return from Mr Clarksons & I *could* almost wish I was with them— What is your Brother Harry doing I do wish that it ⟨was⟩ had been in my power to have got him some appointment that he would have liked but it is now too late in the season the ships were never dispatch'd so early as they are at present—

I shall say nothing about the poems in the 2^{d} vol: of W^{ms} L. B but I wish you would let me known how you like the C. Beggar Joanna Point Rash Judgement & Michael I have sent you poor Mrs Robinsons poems tho I am afraid you will find very little entertainment in them—

Colridge has been shocking ill & I was in great hopes to have seen him before I sail'd our ship comes out of dock on Monday first we are very late but I am in hopes we shall be in the Downs by the 10th of March I have been exceedingly busy preparing my Investment & every thing necessary for sea on my own acct the other ships that sail in the same fleet have been out of dock these three weeks so we shall be, when we come afloat ⟨ ⟩ [2] much hurried with ships business—

Now my dear Mary you must excuse me if I touch a little upon Politics it is reported in town that Mr Pitt has retired or been dismis'd from the administration [3] I am sorry for it as at this critical situation with out it gives us peace it will hurt the country much I only wish they had turn'd him out about 5 or 6 years since—

Do write to me my dear Mary & let me know how you come on at Gallow hill what improvements you have been making &c. c

Remember me kindly to your brother Tom   I am

Yours very Aff^{ly}

John Wordsworth

Staple Inn.

Jany 31st

12. To William Wordsworth

Address: Mr Wordsworth / Mr Clarksons / Penrith / Cumb^{d}

Postmark: A FE 6 [1]801

[11 Staple Inn, February 6, 1801]

My dear W^{m}

I rec^{d} My sisters Letters & have sent Peggy's Letter off with a one pound bank note enclos'd [1]   I am sorry to hear such a bad account of Charles Loyd   I was in hopes from what Christopher said that you would have found him a good neighbour & in particular I remember he said that he was not in the least selfish—& indeed I thought his fault had been that he was too generous—

I am now going to make a request of you which you *may* perhaps think not prudent or proper to comply with.   it is that you will lend me the money which you have in the funds [2]—& I will replace it at the end of the voyage   that is you shall have the same stock whether they have risen or fallen ⟨at the end of⟩ & Rich^{d} will engage to pay you the ⟨m⟩ intrest of the money regularly when I am from home.

Our Ship came out of dock on Monday last & I am in hopes we shall leave Gravesend by this time next month.

You will see Joseph W.[3] at Mr Clarksons & he will have with him the fishing rod I promis'd Mr Simpson, I shall leave some bamboo at My Brothers to be sent to him by the first conveyance—but Mr S will find employment enough in putting the fishing rod I have sent him into some decent shape— I am sorry that Colridge is not coming to town I was in hopes of seeing him I have been with Tobin ⟨who⟩ ^he^ has sent you Bertrams travells I have not seen Stoddart since I last wrote.

I did not like your poem⟨s⟩ of point rash judgement when I first read it—but I have since been excessively pleased with parts of it—& particularly with this part— "that was its horse, its Chariot[4] &c & the whole of that description—& also of the one that follows but Joanna is my favourite poem— I am glad you like the Clarksons so well give my best respects and compliments to them & { }[5] Myers if you see him—

{ } Christopher in town shortly he is to come up as one of the officers of the university to congratulate his Majesty on the *Union*.[6] I have not heard from him since he return'd to Cambridge

Give my kind love to Sara H. & tell Dorothy I shall write to her soon & I am in haste

Yours Affly

John Wordsworth

how is Mary H. I have sent her the L. B. but have not heard whether she has receivd them

Staple Inn

Feby 6th

13. To Mary Hutchinson

Address: Miss Hutchinson / Wykeham / Malton / by York

Postmark: A FE 10 [1]801

[11 Staple Inn,] Monday 8th of Jan [*for* February] [1801]

God love thee my dear Mary I have rec[d] thy kind letter and thank thee most cordially for it & for all the kind and good wishes it contains. I am sorry you have not got the L. B I went immediately to the Coach-house & they told me it had been sent off on sunday week & that they would write by this nights post about it. if you should not get the *vol*[s] by the time you receive this write to me and I will send you down another copy— I knew how rejoiced you would be to receive them on that acc[t] I was angry with myself for not sending them as soon as I might have done— I should be glad to hear that you had got some company or society—& tho you may care very little ab[t] it yourself I do not think on that acc[t] it is the less necessary— I do not mean to say that visiting in the common way is pleasant on the contrary I dislike it very much myself—but even that kind of visiting has its service, for let the people be ever so stupid you may still gather some thing that may entertain or improve—and above all it makes one pleased with ones own home and gives one feelings that one could not otherwise know— *this you may believe I think very fine.*

I wish by some enchantment I could see your improvements at G.[allow] H.[ill] there is not a single *brick* or stone or hedge or plant or *flower* that I would not be delig[h]ted with (⟨it is by the by not I believe the season for flowers⟩) & for her honour Madam Langleys improvements [1] what a pleasure I should take in finding fault with them   the Bridge would either be too large for the pond or too small or too high or too low & then the pond itself would be too large wasting too much good ground or miserably small & then for the plantation (for I suppose her honor ⟨h⟩ cannot do without trees) it would be a vile & harsh mixture of firs and larches chesnuts & poplar willows & laburnums   now by the by how does her honour & its honour behave to you   are they like the lords and ladies I have seen very proud   pray have you got any body that you can *speak* to.

I wish I was once more at Grasmere to see my brother & sister & Sara nor shall I ever fo{rget} the many pleasant hours I have spent there & I look forward with hope and pleasure to the time we shall all meet there—

I should like much to see George upon his farm

I rec^d^ a letter this morning from Dorothy   they are still staying at Mr Clarksons   Coleridge is better   I *was* in hopes to have seen him in town but it is now all over

I am my dear Mary
thine ever affectionately
JOHN WORDSWORTH

/ D° write by return of post

14. To Mary Hutchinson

Address: Miss Hutchinson / Wykeham / Malton / York / *Stamped:* Missent to York / *Written under stamp:* Missent

Postmark: A FE 16 [1]801

[11 Staple Inn, February 16, 1801]

My dear Mary,

I have rec[d] thy last kind letter & thank thee as before also for the honour you have done me in your garden—

now I do request that you will write to me ^(if you have not written)^ immediately and let me know your further opinion of Joanna—Point Rash Judgement & Michael—

I have this evening return'd from vistiting *my* Ship *indeed indeed* she is a most noble one & Gorge himself can never be half so proud as I shall be & O what *a rich dog* they say I am to be   I have had 5.000 £ offer'd for my voyage   What think of that—

It is an ill wind they say that blows no body any good luck   the longer this war continues the better it will be for me—

I am sorry to find that Cole{rid}ge is not coming to town   to be sure I should not have been & [*for* a] *little* glad to have him   I call upon S[t]oddart very often on purpose to have the pleasure of talking about you—   he is a good temper'd man & is writing in W[ms] praise in the British Critic—   I have also seen poor Tobin & like him very much—   you must be acquainted with him at least by name   You will be much displeas'd to find how shockingly misprinted the second vol. of the L. B. is—   When does Tom come home   what is harry doing.   when does George get upon his farm   indeed indeed my dearest Mary there is nothing that thou couldst tell me but I shall be glad to hear and O for a sight of thy dear garden— {I} am glad to hear such a good account of the Langleys— I was afraid they would be much *greater* than they seem to be— how do they come on with ⟨their⟩ the lowland inclosure ground

M^r^ L will find good acc^t^ in it—& it will be of great service to the country in general— by this time *they* are at Grasmere indeed I should like to see my dear friend Sara once more but that cannot be— I rec^d^ a letter from W^m^ this morning he tells me that they walked from Mr Clarksons over the mountains[1] & that they are now going to Keswick I cannot learn from him how long they are to stay at Keswick whether Sara returns or how long she is going to stay with them if she does return— I am afraid they will not have such a good neighbour in Charles L as I could have wishd—

Christopher spoke of him to me in the highest terms

I am thine ever aff^y^

J. Wordsworth

15. To Dorothy Wordsworth

Address: Miss Wordsworth / Ambleside / Kendal / W^t^moreland

Postmark: A FE 21 [1]801

Staple Inn Feby 21st [1801]

My dear Sister,

I rec^d^ a letter from my Uncle W^m^ this morning[1] telling me that they had bought the L. B. ⟨the day⟩ ^some time^

before I sent them down & that they had given one of the copys to Miss Mary [2]

as for the sale of others there can be no doubt but it will be good—but as yet it is impossible to tell whether ⟨al⟩ soon it is likely to [be] rapid— we must see how they are handled by the Reviews

I am out of all patience with the impudence of Longman for only offering 80£ for the LB it is little better than swindling— I am a great man ⟨at Archs'⟩ with Mr Arch tho' he does not know my name— I talk knowin[g]ly of Colrid[g]e Southey. Wordsworth. Lamb &c—

Arch has had a great Sale of the 2^d^ Vol tho I was surprised to find he had sold but few very few of the 2^d^ edition—[3] he ⟨h⟩ said his customers complain'd of ⟨not h⟩ of being cheated out of a preface—[4]

I have been too much engaged to call on Stod[d]art or Tobin— I am order'd to take [leave] of the Court of Directors on Wednesday the 4th of March tomorrow I go down to the ship—& I am obliged every Sunday to be on board— Captn & Mrs W. think no place like bath they will come up to see me off or I believe they would stay there these three months— the⟨ir . . .⟩ [5] Friends Sr W. & Lady Lawson are expected at Bath on the 23^d^ and O the pleasure of being with such great people— I like my officers very much & I have every prospect of having a pleasant & good—voyage

I am Dr Sister Yours ever affectionaly

John Wordswordsworth [6]

Give my kind love to W^m^ and Sara— (in haste)

after I have taken leave of the Court I and [*for* am] not allow'd to stay in {town} I am glad they are in such a hurry {to dis}patch us as it is of the greatest consequence that we should get to China before the Madras & China Ships— it may make a difference of perhaps 30 *p^r^ Cent* in the Sale of our investments— My investment will be ⟨near 10.⟩ between 9 & 10.000£ within these two years there has been such an enormus advance on the price of all European goods that I am af[r]aid we shall not do so well as might be expected but it is all conjecture—

Mary H. has got the L. B. I wrote to her ⟨wishing⟩ desiring to know how she liked different pomems but have not heard f{ro}m her—

16. To Mary Hutchinson

Address: Miss Hutchinson / Wykeham / Malton
Postmark: A FE 24 [1]801

[11 Staple Inn, February 24, 1801]

My dear Mary,

I rec^d^ your letter this morning I am rather anxious to give you my opinion of the L. B. I wish'd to hear ⟨of⟩ your opinion [of] those particular poems which I mention'd before I should speak of them myself— You must know then that P. R. Judgement is not a particular favourite there are some parts of it that in my opinion are written in the true stile of poetry— I like much the description of the thistles beard[1] having so tagged it myself—but the latter part I have thought *too quaint*— Yet I am sure it is a poem that will please many people—

Joanna is by far, far the most beatifull poem W^m^ has ever written of its length it is complete in all its parts— it is written with great tenderness—⟨some humoro⟩ the {descrip}[2]tion of the echo is most admirable— { ha}ve ever read a poem that gave me so {much plea}sure— Your opinion of Michael i{s the same} as my own ⟨Itt⟩ at the first I thoug{ht } rather vulgar which particular[l]y {ought to be} avoided in a blank verse poem—su{ch }es. that he c^{d} look his trouble in the face[3]—th{ese two days, has be}en meat and drink to me[4]—but these objectio{ns I soon go}t the better of— the fathers Speech is { } pathectic—& I like the whole of the pa{ tha}t man grossly errs[5]—& [in] short { } admirable poem— the pet lamb { fav}ourite of mine W^{m} had Joanna in {mind when} he wrote that poem[6] you do not {mention} Ruth which has offended me greatly {It is a} favourite of mi{ne }[7] I must { }[8]

I'll tell you by & by what I think *is* & what is likely to be the opinion of the public of these poems ⟨& the⟩ at present I have not time— Give my kind remembrances to Tom I am sorry Harry has got no employment for it is the devil for any man of even common feeling to hanghing upon his friends I am glad you accepted ⟨ ⟩[9] Madame L. present by taking it you *indirectly* conferr'd an obligation upon her—& of course I am much pleased to hear that she is so kind to you— I should suppose that George would be worse than Betty Foy[10] till he gets holds of his farm & for three months afterwards—

I am order'd to take leave of the Court of directors this day Week—& I hope we shall leave Engl^{d} by the latter end of March

I am My dear Mary in great haste
thine affectionate Friend
JOHN WORDSWORTH

Feb^{r} 24th

17. To Mary Hutchinson

Address: Miss Hutchinson / Wykeham / Malton / ⟨ ⟩
Postmark: ⟨ ⟩ FE 27 [1]801

[11 Staple Inn, February 25 and 26, 1801]

My dear Mary,

As my time is precious I think I cannot do better than by writing to *thee* & more particularly so as I was so short in my last letter— Cottle [1] had no *hand* in the correction of the press it was entrusted to Mr Davy [2] whom I suppose you must have heard of he is a great Chemist at Bristol— I like your criticism of Michael & except the Language which you do not mention it has had the same effect upon me—

the Danish Boy does not at all intrest me it is meant as a *wild* story and dream of Fancy— You ask me what impression these vols have made the fact is every one is so full of his own business that *even I* scarce hear them mention'd except I *lug* them in myself.—

when the Reviews come out we shall know more abt them— I was with Stodd{art} this morning who is writing in a *friendly* way for t{he Bri}tish critic— I saw the Review of them which he had {wr}i{tt}en & it did not pl[e]ase me I thought it too indiscriminately flattering he says he has shewn it to the Reviewers & they approve of his review—but will make some small alterations— I think in time they will become popular but it will be by degrees— the fact is there are not a great many that will be pleased with the poems but those that are pleased will be pleased in a high degree & they *will be people of sense* this will have weight—& people who neither understand or wish to understand will buy & praise them— Longman is a vile abominable and impudent Jew for only giving W^m^ 80£ for the 2 Editions[3] he will clear at least 400£ or perhaps 500£. they are sure of a good and steady sale—

I suppose by this time *they* will be thinking of returning to Grasmere—[4] I am glad W^m^ have given up all thoughts of going to {Kesw}ick. I suppose you know that Calvert offer'd them {his hou}se at Windy Brow—[5]

how am I to direct to you am I to say Wykeham ⟨by Yo⟩

I am orderd to take leave of the Court of Directors this day week most of the commanders of our fleet leave to day after that I shall only be allow'd to stay in town four days & I hope we shall leave Gravesend by this day fortnight— write to me often and *long* letters I am now getting so much out of my regular line that you cannot expect to hear ⟨of m⟩ from me at all times so soon as I could wish I have a dozen letters to write in a day & this you may believe is no small task to one who dislikes that business as much as I do— I make this request because my dear Mary there is nothing that thou canst write but what will give me pleasure & to be with *thee* I read thy letters over a *dozen* times in a day—
Good night & believe me to be thine affectionate friend.

JOHN WORDSWORTH

Wednesday night. 25th of Febr Staple Inn—

Thursday morning. I have recd a Letter from Dorothy this morning Sara is staying at Keswick but will return to Grasmere where she will remain abt a month, Coleridge is better—W^m^ says that the nutting and Joanna shew the greatest genious of any poems in the 2d Vol Joanna is indeed a most delightful poem it is my greatest favourite it is a perfect poem has a beginning middle—and end—[6]

Kitt is very much pleased [with] the poems—

God Bless you farewell

18. To Dorothy Wordsworth

Address: Miss Wordsworth / Ambleside / Kendal / Westmorland

Postmark: ⟨ ⟩ FE 27 [1]801

[11 Staple Inn, February 26, 1801][1]

My dear Dorothy,

I rec[d] your letter this morning & enclosed I send you a one pound note ⟨which⟩ ^out of it^ you will give to Molly (10.6)— You may tell W[m] I shall send him down a new silk hat & the old one I had at Grasmere tho' upon 2[d] consideration I am afraid it will be too small & all the old clothes I can muster—[2] Ric[d] will also send what he can spare— as for the Telescope I cannot yet promise it to you I will see first whether I shall want it— it is of a very convenient size for ship board and particularly in a fleet where we must be constantly looking out for signals— let me know whether Peggy has rec[d] the one pound note I sent her— I am sorry I cannot let you have any money ⟨f . . .⟩[3] ^before I leave england^ or provide for you more than the ten pounds every six months— a Guinea is of more consequence to me now than 20 will [be] at the end of two voyages— I suppose there is little doubt but that I shall make at least 6.000£ this voyage but it is a heavy drawback borrowing money—& taking goods very disadvantageously on acc[t] of not having money—so that when I once get the command of ten thousand pound I shall *do,* our China voyages are now most excellent I suppose Captn Wordsworth made 15.000 last voyage—

You must remember me to the Simpsons & tell old Mr Simpson I have got a piece of bamboo ready to send him when I can find a proper conveyance it may perhaps be sent with the old clothes— I am afraid the old clothes will be bad enough perhaps not worth the carriage—

I am glad to hear that Coleridge is better, I call'd yesterday on Stoddart & he said that he had rec'd a letter from Colridge about the L. B. desiring that I might call at Longmans to know if they had been sent— I was there this morning & was inform'd by Rees that they had gone off a month ago—that is immediately after they were publish'd— I am sorry Fox has not answered W^ms^ letter [4] it was the only one of much importance— I suppose he is thinking & most likely intresting himself in the Ministerial changes— [5] it appears by the papers he is living with L. Fitzwilliam [6] the King is very poorly. at this time it is certainly unfortunate— I shall leave town to join the ship in about ten days of course I am very busy & you must not expect to hear so regularly from me as I could wish.— When I am on board & clear of Gravesend I shall write to you often— I am employ'd all day in shipping men, & with Tradesmen of every discription ⟨so⟩ & being a new thing I find myself a little ⟨aw⟩ at a loss— I do not go on so well as an old experienced Capt. would do— I should like to have a sight of your little garden but that is impossible

Give my kind love to W^m^ & Sara
I am Your Aff^t^ {Brother
JOHN WORDSWORTH}

19. To Dorothy Wordsworth

Address: Miss Wordsworth / Ambleside / Kendal / W^t^moreland / *Readdressed on flap, in another hand:* S. T. Coleridge Esqr / Greta Hall / Keswick
Postmark: A [M]R 2 [1]801

[11 Staple Inn, March 2, 1801]

My dear Dorothy,

Stoddarts review of W^ms^ Poems came out to day, with some small additions and alterations— he says of Joanna—Perhaps the English language can boast few instances of descriptive poetry, enlivened with a happier variety of imagery than the fanciful echo in the poem inscribed to Joanna— The Ladys laugh to be sure is loud, but it is not unpleasing— is there not a falling off?" [1] this is all that is said of the poem— Upon the whole I think the review will do considerable good he says but the most singular specimens of unpretending yet irresistible pathos are the two Songs p. 50 & 52, in artlessness they strongly remind us of Burns—but perhaps go beyond him in delicacy— as they have a secret connection we shall insert both—Strange fits &c She dwelt among &c—

⟨this⟩ ^The following^ is the end of the Review I { } [2] ⟨not⟩ ^I believe not^ by Stoddart— When the art of poetry has been long cultivat{ed} among a polishd people & brought to a state of great refinement the natural operations of an ill judged ambition to excel even those who have most successfully adorned the language—leads writers either to employ an affected and over labour'd style or at least to keep upon the high stilts of elegance to the exclusion of ⟨it⟩ nature and simplicity— In such a state of the poetic art that man may be considerd as a public

benefactor who with talents equal to the task which is arduous recals attention to the more natural style & shews what may be effected by simple language expressive of human passions & genuine not artificial feelings—
In this character Mr W. appears—& appears with a success to which we could by no means refuse our approbation—

We will not deny that some times he goes so far in his pursuit of simplicity as to become flat or weak—but in general he has set an example which the full dress'd poet of affectation might wish but wish in vain to follow—

We would correct Mr W. as the dancing master of Hogarth would correct the attitude of Antinous— here ende{th the} chapter—

the other parts of th{e revi}ew speak much in praise of the poems

I expect Captn & Mrs Wordsworth in town from Bath this evening— I am to take leave the day after to-morrow but I am afraid we shall not sail so soon as I could wish—

the bales which we are to take ⟨ ⟩[3] are not ready—

it is a pity as it is of great consequence to get out as soon as possible— the days are getting long, which is a great comfort— short [*for* long] nights in the Channel are bad— W^ms poems are not reviewed in any of the other Reviews Give my kind love to W^m & Sara &

I am Yours Aff^ly
JOHN WORDSWORTH

Staple Inn March 2^d 1801—

20. To Mary Hutchinson

Address: Miss Hutchinson / Wycombe / Malton / Yorkshire

Postmark: B MR 9 [1]801

[11 Staple Inn,] Monday [March 9, 1801] [1]

My dear Mary,

I came up from the Ship yesterday evening for the last time till I join her for good— I do not known the day I am to leave London but I suppose it will be about Friday. We are doing well on board & I have every prospect of [a] good voyage & the ship is a most most noble one— the officers I like well they are very good *young men* the eldest about three & twenty—but I do not like them the worse for that they will be more *obedient* & less *knowing*— the Midshipmen are the finest lads I ever saw We have eight—& our Ships Company will consist of about 180 Men & 32 Guns—*18 pounders* & *twelves* now I hope I have made a sailor of you We could mount 70 Guns if we could only muster men for them—

What you say about Michael is perfectly right & there certainly ought to be a difference between What the poet is supposed to say himself & what—the character says— now that he could ⟨not⟩ look &c: is what the poet says & therefore objectionable—but the other tho certainly low is in the (meat & Drink) character of the man—[2] I am glad you like Joanna so well it is my first favourite when I said that it was written with tenderness I meant that it concluded with tenderness— the other parts may be seen by: the nature of the poem— You must not speak so high[l]y of my judgement &c you'll make me too vain— as for P. R. J. tho' at the first I did not like the poem it has improv'd much upon me & after I had written so harshly against it my heart misgave me—for ⟨it⟩ I began to like it very much tho' I think it a very inferior poem to Joanna I am glad to hear that you are such a great favourite with the Langleys it will be a pleasant change & will show you the follys weakness & vanity of all great people— I like the Langleys better than any rich people I {kno}w they were so good to the poor in letting them put their cows in to the Park— it was not so good in the act itself as in the example— I remember I was much pleased with it & thought well of them for it. so different to that haughty pride that cannot bear to see a poor man them [*for* there]— on that acc^{t} I was anxious to hear that they had taken ⟨at⟩ notice of you—and more particularly so as you were strangers in the country— I cannot express how glad I should be to see thee and thy dear garden with all its improvements—nor how I wish in *the form of a spirit* to hear your & her honours consultations I am in great haste my dearest Mary thine affectiont friend

John Wordsworth

If I have time I will write again tomorrow or the day after— Do let me hear from you it is scarce fair to expect such a long letter as the last from this short scrawl but you must take compassion upon me & consider that at this time I [am] much hurried—

pray what did you mean in your letter by scratching out ⟨Wycombe⟩ leaving Malton & ⟨York⟩—

21. To Mary Hutchinson

Address: Miss Hutchinson / Wycombe / Malton / Yorkshire

Postmark: ⟨ ⟩ MR 12 [1]80[1]

[11 Staple Inn,] Monday Evening [and Tuesday evening, March 9 and 10, 1801]

I wrote to you this evening but I cannot forgo the pleasure of talking a little to you again the post office is shut up at 6 o'Clock & I am generally in the city till 4 oClock so that it leaves me only two hours to write my letters & get my Dinner— I should like to shake hands with your friend the Clergy man at Hutton Bushel[1]—& the *Doctor* you say nothing of him he made *me* many kind offers in the hunting line— I was to have had the whole grounds [of] St John [and] St Ledger to myself— I do not think that W^ms^ poetry will become popular for some time to come it certainly does not suit the present taste I was in company the other evening with a gentleman he read the Beggar[2] "Why says he this is very pretty but you may call it any [thing] but poetry— I like the description but still it is very different to what I should conceive poetry to be— I said it might be true (for I like to give people their own way) & that perhaps from local circumstances I might be more interested in it than it deserved— the truth is there are few people that like, or read, poetry many who buy it—buy it for the name—read about twenty lines the language is very fine & they are content with praising extravagantly the whole poem— Most of W^ms^ poetry improves upon 2^d^ 3 or 4th reading now people in general are not sufficiently interested with the first reading to induce them to try a 2^d^— Tuesday evening— I rec^{d} a letter from Dorothy this morning with the complimentary letters of Messrs Lewis &c: c. copyed by Sara & a most entertaining copy of verses by Mr Lewis ∧these verses were sent as Nonparriel to W^{m}.∧

the convict of W$^{m's}$ is *nothing* compared to Lewis'—[3]

I am sorry to find that Sara is soon to leave Grasmere I understand that George will carry her away in about a fortnight— it will be a great loss to *them*—

You must give my Kind Love to George when you write him he is a great favourite of mine— ⟨You⟩ there are great changes taking place at Grasmere you remember the fir trees upon the hill by the cottage that over looks (or rather the fir trees) ∧that overlook)∧ the lake of Grasmere ∧upon the road to Rydale above my B^{r} house [4]∧—they are cut down I wish I had the *monster* that cut them down in *my* ship & I would give him a tight flogging—

I like Coleridges Love ⟨very⟩ ∧⟨mucch⟩∧ indeed I have been much pleased with it—but accor*ding to my taste* it ⟨is not a poem that I like⟩ is of a species of poetry that I do not like— it is very different to the whole vol^{s} you say that the antient M—is now ⟨symbol⟩ [5] void of obscurity [6] as for my part it is a poem that I could never bear to read— I dare say it is beatiful but I cannot see the beauty— the Nightingale is a great favourite & the language is certainly most beautiful

our ship will sail from Gravesend I hope about this day week but you will direct to me at my Brothers till you hear more from me— I shall be obliged to leave town *for good* abt {Friday} or Saturday every thing at present goes well with me— Captn & Mrs Wordsworth came up from Bath last week they have been much delighted with the place they came up on purpose to see me off I was with them at the ship on Sunday they will afterwards go to Cumberland— Capt. ⟨Wordsworth⟩ & Mrs. W. are as good people as ever lived they seem & without affectation to be much intrested in W^ms^ *Welfare*—

God love thee my dearest Mary & believe me to be thy affectionate friend—JOHN WORDSWORTH

The person of whom I spoke in the beginning of [the] letter did not know at the time who had written the poems he spoke from his own feelings & Ideas of poetry he is of the class of Loshs's of Carlisle [7] if you ever heard of them— Indeed my brother's poetry has a great deal to struggle [against] but I hope it will overcome all— it is certainl{y} founded upon nature—& that is the best foundation— Mr Losh is a great favourite with my brother but that do not hit upon this point—

I am glad to find that C. it [*for* is] better— his Child is got quite well—[8]

22. To Dorothy Wordsworth

Address: Miss Wordsworth / Ambleside / Kendall / W^t^moreland

Postmark: B MR 12 [1]801

[11 Staple Inn, March 10, 1801]

My dear Dorothy,

I rec^d^ your Letter this morning with Sara's Copy of Letters & you must give my kind kind love and thanks to her I was much entertaind with the contents & Mr Lewis's poem is the most funny one I ever read—it is quite a caricature of its kind— they ought to have made a parson of him instead of a M. P— [1] the telescope [2] is a small handy one & I cannot now spare it I have got much better glasses but none that will suit my convenience so well— I am glad Molly has improved so much upon your hands she will save you a great deal of money & I hope she will have her health— I had I [*for* a] very very kind letter from Sally Lowthian [3] the other day—& such a one from Peter Crosthwaite [4] as would do your heart good to see— I have sent it to Captn W. or I would have given you an extract—but he speaks in the highest terms of the *glory &* honour to which the W'^{s} have arrived—with a long list of things that I am to get for him—which he *has promisd to pay me* handsomely for— I am sorry you have not heard from Peggy but I hope she has got the money— [5] what made me more anxious to hear was that I had given the letter to a waiter at a Coffeehouse ‸to put into the post office‸ & was a little afraid on that acc^{t}— You must suppose that I should not be a *little* rejoiced to see you at Grasmere it is a place that is most dear to me & I hope you will never leave it— What a most sacrilegious Monster that was that caused the fir trees to be cut down near that delightful cottage— I cannot bear to think of it— I have not heard from Kitt since he went to cambridge but perhaps it may be my fault I have not written to him— I think I am sorry for ⟨t⟩his connection [with] Miss L.[loyd] thoughs ⟨ ⟩ ‸⟨she . . .⟩ ⟨ ⟩‸ [6] a fine looking woman she talk'd a good deal when I was with her—but *I* was *most eloquent*— [7] upon the whole there was *that something* in her countenance that I could not bear to like— [8] I think that you Sara &

W^{m} altogether will not have courage to attack Mr Benson [9] in the way that would suit him—& indeed if you had it would be useless— I am sorry for your poor old neighbours that they are at last come to the parish [10] I have seen Stoddart this morning by some unaccountable mistake the poems have not reach'd him I carried Bertrams Travels to Longman—& he promis'd me faithfully that the peoms should it be sent at the same time—the Travels were sent to Longmans after the poems were publish'd

I return'd from the ship yesterday [I] am of course very busy & shall leave town on Friday *for good* Captn & Mrs W. came up from ⟨town on⟩ ‸Bath‸ last week on purpose to see me off & they were at the ship on Sunday You will see them in Cumb^{d} shortly they are much delighted with W^{ms} poems & ⟨ ⟩ [11] & Mrs Words. thanks W^{m} most cordially for his letter [12] You had better direct to me at Staple Inn till you hear from me— I cannot conceive what can detain your letters so long upon the road The last but one which I rec^{d} was dated the 24 of Feb^{r} & I did not receive it till the 9th of March I shall take care that the clothes are sent d{own} before I leave town—

I am sorry you are going to loose Sara so so{on} you will ⟨ ⟩ [13] ‸have‸ a great loss— You must remember me to my *old friend* George— I should like to see him admiring the beauties of Nature at Grasmere—

remmember me to Colridge—& the Simpsons I have got a piece of Bamboo which I shall desire to be sent with the old clothes—

I am My dear Sister Yours ever Aff^{ly}

JOHN WORDSWORTH

I have seen very little of the Myers' they live all most constantly with Mr Robinson[14] at Sion hills—

I write in great haste & you must excuse mistakes

[*At head of letter, upside down:*] *It* would delight me to find which touches of poetry Mr L. could introduce into his poem—

[*On back of letter, cancelled:*] ⟨My dear Dorothy⟩

23. To Mary Hutchinson

Address: Miss Hutchinson / Wykeham / Malton / Yorkshire

Postmark: B MAR 17 1801

[Ship *Earl of Abergavenny,* Gravesend,]
March 16th [1801]

My dear Mary I have just time to say that I am now on b^{d} the Abergany for good and all— I wish you would write to me immediately & direct to Staple Inn to be forwarded

We shall leave gravesend ab^{t} Thursday & shall proceed to the down[s] as quick as possible I am My Dearest Mary Yours Aft^{y}

JOHN WORDSWORTH

24. To Dorothy Wordsworth

Address: {Miss Wordsworth} / Ambleside / Kendal / Westmorland
Postmark: Missing

The Weather is fine & the breezes freshenjng You may soon expect to hear of our arrival at *Portsmouth*

Downs
28th [and 29th] of March [1801]

My dear Dorothy,

We are arrived safe in the Downs & are waiting for a fair wind to carry us to Portsmouth— At present every thing goes well with us & I trust it will continue to *do so*—

You can have no idea of the trouble I have had in procuring men for the ship of the tricks that have been played me by running away [1] &c. C. if we loose not more than 500£. in the manning of our ship I shall be satisfied—

Sunday 29th

I recd your Letter of the 24th this morning I am sorry to find you are going to loose Sara she will indeed be a great loss to you you must give my very kind kind Love & remembrances ⟨to her⟩ when you write to her for I suppose she will have left you by this time—

I was myself exceedingly angry at the misprinting of the L. B. & complain'd to Rees [2] of it who did not seem to trouble himself much about it—but I hope it will not much injure the sale of them there is no doubt but they will soon get into another edition—

As for Stoddart you must not expect to hear from him he is so much engaged in his own compositions that he has scarse time to speak to a person that calls upon him— he wrote to me a note when I was in the greatest hurry of my business just before I left town & when I had papers of the greatest importance to settle, requesting that I—would go to Longman to inquire about the L. B &c— I declined it because I was certain he could have no engagements half so pressing as my own— & in the 2^{d} place out of an act of civility he ought to have done it himseft— he is going to publish a book of his own & every one must be anxious for his own child, but if I may judge, he carries it to too great an extent—

You made me quite melancholy this morning ab^{t} Coleridge— I fear he will have bad very bad health & it grieves me to think that he should be throwing himself away— poor Hartly I hope he will live to see many a winter & many a summer pass over his head [3] he is a most ‸uncommon &‸ delightful boy I am glad to hear that W^{m} is *going on* with the recluse [4] that he may have his health & inclination to proceed will be my constant wish— You ask me about the poems in the 2^{d} Vol. I have read Michael to several pe{rsons} [5] & they all even at the first reading have been more af{fected} with it than the Brothers & for my part I now {like} it much better it is indeed a most superior poem{—}

I like Mathew ⟨much⟩ better than I used to do but {it is} *no great favourite*— the Peom that has the m{ost effect} upon me is Lucy Gray—‸indeed I think that a most de{lightful poem}‸ the next Mathew {though in} a much inferior degree— the rest I mean {those that} were written when I was at Grasmer{e } [6] the same feelings as ⟨they used to do⟩ { } Point Rash Judgement has become a {favourite} ⟨with me⟩ but Joanna & Emma {I like} most in their different ways— I have written to Kitt but have ne{ver } Lett{er i}f he has left

Cambridge {   } him—   no doubt he must go to {   } Loyds   I hate the very name of {   }   I am certain they will never {   } & it appears to me t{   } ⟨ ⟩ great disservice t{   } of their description {   } ^& friendly^ terms ⟨with them⟩ {   } in a considerable {   } last can never hav{e   } & therefore it would {   } known them—   as {for the L. B. give your}self no uneasiness ab{out their making their} own way—   they cannot, nor must you expect that {they} will meet with their due praise or reward ⟨at⟩ {*imme*}*diately*—   the *errors,* will soon be rectified & all {be as you wi}sh—yet I would particularly recomend that {you} publish nothing without correcting the press {yourself} in future—

{   } & we are just setting {   } shall be tomorrow {   } in the Downs   {remembe}r me aff^y^ to {   }

JOHN WORDSWORTH

{29}th of March

25. To Dorothy Wordsworth

Address: Miss Words{worth / Grasmer}e / {Amblesi}de / Westmoreland / Single
Postmarks: POR{TS}M{OU}TH; G APR 11 1801

[Portsmouth,] April 2^d^ [through April 9], 1801

My dear Sister,

We arrived here on the 31^t^ of March & it is reported that we are likely to sail ab^t^ this time next week if the wind should be fair   I wish it may be true, the fleet that I was in hopes we should have sailed with we had the mortification to pass as we came into Portsmouth— to loose a fair wind and to be obliged to anchor in this place to lay God knows how long is truly mortifying— I have nothing to say to you that can be the least intresting a more stupid place than a ship cannot well be imagined—except that you will be pleased to hear that we have had a most delightful passage from the Downs & that in every respect I am as much pleased with the officers &c c of the ship—& have as fair a prospect before [me] as any man could wish for—

I have been on shore this afternoon to strech my legs upon the Isle of White— the ^evening^ Primroses are beatiful—& the daisy's ⟨in the⟩ ^after sunset^ are like little *white* stars upon the dark green fields— [1] how very far inferior is this Island to the Lakes in the North of England— Yet in many respects this place is most exceedingly intresting. as a Landscape the rich wodds & fine bay, the intrest that one must always feel from the ships & *Life* there is upon water—the noise of seamen in the evening heard at a distance the boat men & fishermen near the shore—& then on shore for it is ⟨most⟩ the place of resort to all those who are going to India come in the highest spirits upon the thoughts of leaving England others parting with their wives fathers or nearest relations perhaps to remain in India for many years & never to see them again—⟨and⟩ the different countenances ⟨the different⟩ are truly intresting—*too often disgusting.*—

Sad how very diffrent are the manners of the poor people from those in the North of England— Peter Crosthwaite himself would not wish to extort more from the Nobility that come to visit the Lakes than one [of] the boatmen here would do ^to a poor man^ going off to a ship in fact they rise in demand according to your necessities—that is for ab^{t} three miles if your are in a great hurry to get off to the ship they charge you three guineas if in a very great hurry four & if you must be off to the ship just as much as they like that is from 4. to 10 Guineas—

the poor people ⟨here⟩ are not to blame I only lament they should have such means of corruption— as long as the war continues they will find a good harvest in our E^{t} India gentry I only hope & trust that in the North of England you will never have a set of men supported by visitors to the Lakes— they will be the very ruin & ⟨ ⟩ the hearts ruin of the country— April the 7th My dear Dorothy Since writing the above I have rec^{d} your two Letters with Sara's copy of W^{ms} poems —& since that time I have been on shore troubled with a set of the greatest rascals that ever livd I do not mean that they have hurt me ⟨nor⟩ or are likely to hurt *me* but to see the depravity of the men that we have to deal with is truly shocking— now I will give you one instance, I have had an action for 25£ pound brought against me (that is the ship) merely because the man thinks that rather than be troubled with his impertinence I will pay him three or four Guineas—

In answer to your *long* letters I scarce know where to begin in the first place your story of the Sea{man's} Mother[2] was affecting just what human nature ^is &^ *ought* to be— the sailors are allowed and particularly in merchant ships to carry birds ⟨I have seen them ^wish to^ bring monkeys on b^{d} but were not allow'd but in most ships even in our s{ervi}ce on . . . of ships . . . is allow'd—& tho . . . they . . . particularly . . . —⟩ & they are more fond of them than other men

I do not know what to think or say ab^{t} W^{ms} heal{t}h

I only hope he will have good spirits & bear up under the {pa}in he may suffer as much as possible & I hope that he suffers nothing from lowness of ⟨ ⟩y spirits in consequence of Montague [3] as I am placed in such a situation that I can always ha{ve it} in my power to assist him but the longer I keep back the better it will be for all of us— [4] Give my kind love & thanks to sara for the trouble she has had— by this time your cold ^& eyes^ *must* be better how in the name of goodness came you to be so unwell with these colds, is the house damp! this I must particularly recomend that you do not walk out with out being perfectly defended about your feet I have suffer'd the most excrusiating torment (not on b[d] of ship) from the rheumatism which I think was caused by wearing thin shoes in London after the thick ones & worsted stocking in the country— [5] it is { } [6] tell what I have felt, it is now god be thank'd all over—

the pain came upon me at one oClock in the morning after I had got warm in bed & continued till 7— in the day time I was perfectly well it was an intermittant Rheumatic fevor— I had if [*for* it] for two months & was at last obliged to apply to a Physician who gave me great relief—

We are painting the ship and making all as smart Never ship was like us— indeed we are not a *little* proud—

I do not think we shall leave portsmouth before this day fortnight. We have not yet rec[d] our dispatches from the India house—

I hope to god your Cold is better I wish you could send me the first part of the poem [7] give my kindest Remembrances to Colridge & the Simpsons & to old Molly I am delighted to hear you speak so well of her—

do write to me upon the receipt of this letter at Portsmouth   I do not think the ship will have sail'd

Give my kind love to W^m & I am
Your Aff Brother
JOHN WORDSWORTH

April 9th In great haste)

26. To Mary Hutchinson

Address: Miss Hutchinson / Wykeham / Malton / Yorkshire
Postmarks: PORTSMOUTH; G APR 11 1801

[Portsmouth, c. April 9, 1801]

You will be pleased my dear Mary to hear that we are arrived safe at Portsmouth   we had a most delightful passage round from Gravesend—   I expect we shall receive our dispatches from the India house on Saturday [1] & then we shall sail with the first fair wind & the sooner it comes the better on many accounts, it is very unpleasant to be laying here in suspence—   When we arrived at Portsmouth we had the mortification to pass the last fleet that sailed with a fine fair breeze & we were obliged to Anchor to lay god knows how long—   I think it is likely that we may remain here at least a fortnight—but however it is all uncertain—as so much depends upon the winds—

pray my dearest mary how long is it since you took me to be a conjurer   by what enchantment do you suppose that I could find out that there was any thing omitted in Michael— [2]   I did not at first like the poem so much as I expected   indeed I was *disapointed* when I first read it having heard much of it from Stoddart who at the same time knew no more about it except to praise it than a goose— I rather think he praisd it because he had heard Colridge speak highly of it— it is now my first and greatest favourite— what has surprizd me the most is that those of my acquaintance who have read the Brothers & Michael have been more affected by Michael at the first reading— I think it is a far more ⟨t⟩ pathectic [poem] than the brothers but not so striking at the first I am speaking according to my own feelings— I had a letter from my sister indeed two ^for one was sent to the Downs & the ship had sail'd.^ since I came here inclosing two large & ful sheets of poetry unpublish'd of W^{ms} & copied by sara the last one ⟨the⟩ was the very last thing she did at Grasmere I shall keep them for ever for her sake—

When you write and see her say every thing that is kind for me— I am sorry to find from my sister's Letter that W^{ms} health is but very indifferent ^& that he finds himself unable to go on with any work^ & Colridges prospect from a very bad constitution or habit of body is not better —& from the expences of a family he is obliged to employ himself in a way which is unworthy of him—that is in writing for Newspapers &c—

Indeed it is a most melancholy thing to think that either of them should want ^a reasonable share of^ money considering the times—that W^{ms} health should be hurt by anxiety which I fear it is—that C. should be obliged to write for Newspapers *I am truly sorry* for the fate of your poor old dog[3] poor thing I remember it very well— What can make your brother Harry think of going to America it is a most detestable place & I would advise him to stay at home rather than go there has he any friends in America— it is my belief that for an Englishman no place is equal to England—

this I am certain of that the Americans are a bad race— —much worse than they are represented to be—

Give my comp^s to ⟨my⟩ ^our^ friend the Stewart at Hackness [4] & tell him I shall bring home some rare China flowers & plants to decorate his garden— he shall have the tea tree with a couple of chinese figures (mandarins) instead of Harlequin & Columbine— that thy flowers & plants & c may live & prosper will be the constant wish of thine affectionate Friend

J. Wordsworth

Give my kind remembrances to Tom: & also to Harry if he be with you. I shall write to you once more before the ship sails. now I do request & insist that you will write to me at St Helena [5] & I shall *occasionally* write to you in the course of the passage if I have means but that is uncertain— send your Letter to my brothers desiring it on the back to be put into the India house—

27. To Dorothy Wordsworth

Address: Miss Wordsworth / Ambleside / Kendal / W^t moreland

Postmarks: PORTSMOUTH; G APR 24 1801

Ship El of Abergavenny [Portsmouth,] April the 22 [and 23, 1801]

We have the finest ship in the fleet she is indeed a most noble ship and is the *pride* of the fleet & the Service— nobody can tell her from a 74 Gun Ship—

My dear Sister,

I have rec^d both your letters & am most truly sorry to

hear of poor Coleridge— I am convinced that nothing would do him good but a warm climate—& yet I cannot tell what place to recommend— St Michaels [1] is the most healthy island in *the world.* Yet I am afraid he could get no accomodation and particularly for his family— the person I sail'd with to St Michaels *is gone to the Devil*—and the Merchant with whom I lived ⟨has also⟩ at St Michaels has also *quarrel'd* with the owners of the ship at Wthaven, & now I believe they have no connection with [the] Island— of this I am certain that it would be very imprudent in Colridge to take Mrs Col: with him till he has seen the place— the Baths I am certain & confident would cure him—

If Col. goes from Wthaven this must be the plan, write to Captn W. or you will see him very shortly & he will make intrest with the merchants at Wthaven for Col:s Accomodation upon the Island supposing there is a ship going to St Michaels— they have no inns & I was inform'd that a single person could lodge very comfortably at one of the *convents* for abt 15£ pr an yet the only way would be to get recomended to some Merchant upon the Island I found them very hospitable & if it was only for going the voyage ⟨for⟩ the benefit of the sea air it would be of service to him—if he is sufficiently strong to undertake it— Captn W. will have it more in his power to serve him at Wthaven than me— indeed I can do nothing— my reason for not telling you that I was unwell in London was that I forgot it— during the day I was as well and *lookd* as well as man could do consequently I forgot all my complaints in the day— the fever came on at one oClock in the morning & lasted till seven & in truth gave me a pretty squeezing it was occasioned by wet feet the yarn stocking[s] and thick shoes—was such a change to fine silk stockings & thin shoes— at present I have most excellent health & am likely to continue so—

I thank you for the poems you have copied— I always liked the preface to Peter Bell [2] & would be obliged if you could send it to me— the female vagrant ⟨I did not⟩ I have not yet read with corrections [3] ⟨I shall have . . . ⟩ [4] I was much pleased with the corrections in the ⟨2^{d}⟩ in the poem⟨s⟩ to Col: [5] the beginning of what Sara copied is very much improved and I liked the poem altogether much better than at Grasmere indeed I have been exceedingly pleased with it & it continues to improve upon me— as for the L. B. I never give myself the smallest concern about them I am certain in time they *must sell*—

I had almost forgot Kitt— I think I am sorry f{or} him— [6] as for Charles Loyd he is a most incomprehensible Knave and ass to deceive his father & can be a man of no principle— I am sorry to say I cannot tell when we shall sail the Bengal fleet are going tomorrow yet we ⟨are⟩ have not rec^{d} our dispatches tho' ⟨we⟩ the ships ⟨are all here⟩ of our fleet are all here— it is reported that we are to take out troops to Batavia [7] I should not be surprized if we were to remain here these three weeks indeed I can not comprehend the cause of our delay—

the 23^{d} the Bengali fleet have sailed with a fine breeze & left us behind you must write to Rich^{d} about the box of old clothes.[8] I shall write to him to—

The L. B. are in almost every Booksellers shop in Portsmouth—which has surprized me because they deal as little in new books at Portsmouth as an[y] town in England of its size I am going to buy a copy here— the corrections [9] I have not yet got but expect them by the Purser. I shall write to you again before we sail Give my love to W^m^ & I am

Your Affectionate Brother
JOHN WORDSWORTH

28. To Mary Hutchinson

Address: Miss Hutchinson / Wykeham / Malton / Yorkshire
Postmarks: PORTSMOUTH; G MAY 8 1801 [1]

Ship Abergavenny
Portsmouth
May the 2nd [1801]

My dearest Mary,

Our Ship is not yet off & I am dying with vexation at being detained the Bengal fleet saild last week & we have been left behind & the wind has continued fair for this fortnight our *Pursers* have been ⟨wait⟩ in daily attendance at the Indiahouse & have not yet ⟨ ⟩ [2] rec^d^ their dispatches we may still remain here a month— there is comfort for you— I think that if we are [not] dispatched the W^tn^ winds will soon set in & keep us here —God knows how long. come I will compound for a month— I am rather *of an easy temper* and also have the pleasing satisfaction of having some of my friends in the same predicament with myself or I believe I should go mad— O. the blessed uncertainty of a Sea life—

come come my dearest Mary do not tell me again that you do not know how to direct to me ⟨that⟩ do you suppose that J. W Esqr &c. c is not to be found in such a place as Portsmouth— if you were to see how great a man I am on b^{d} my great ship you would say that I have just cause to be offended— direct to me at Staple Inn when you write to me at St Helena to be forwarded—

I have not rec^{d} a letter of any kind from any one that I care for—for this last fortnight— I suppose you all think I am half way to China by this time indeed this is a most stupid place to be in— my brother *Commanders* are *dashing* away in high style on shore this I could never bear was my fortune ever so large I remain constantly on b^{d} & have become quite an *alien* to them— I ⟨have⟩ am beginning to read Shakespears works & cannot express how much I have been affected by Othello with shocking faults Shakespear carries you beyond the bound of human nature— he is the greatest of all great men— Romeo & Juliet was the first I began with Juliet's character is most incomparably drawn but how far how very far is that play inferior to Othello—

Write to me immediately & If I should not receive it here ⟨send . . . ⟩ [3] you may assure it to be return'd I ⟨ ⟩ [4] shall write to Dorothy tomorrow I wrote some time since but I suppose she thinks we have saild— *Dear* Sara's copy of W^{ms} poetry I read with great delight both for her sake & for the ⟨ ⟩ [5] past remembrances it calls to my mind— I shall write to thee again my dear Mary before the ship sails whether I hear from thee or not & by every opportunity that offers God love thee —& believe me to be thine affectionate Friend

JOHN WORDSWORTH

Saturday the 2^{d} of May—

This not being a post night I cannot send the letter

off you cannot conceive how anxious I am to {get} away It is in a thousand instances desireable we shall lose our proper passage, I am laying here at an enormous expence, & it is to me the dullest of all dull places.

we shall be 17 or 20 months over our voyage instead of 12 the Madras & China ships will get to China before us and spoil our Markets—& yet upon the whole I *really* care as little about it as man can do—yet it is tedidious & provoking— I went on shore yesterday morning to see if W[ms] books were review'd in the Monthly Review when I got there I found the Reviews did [not] come down till the Evening so I came on b[d] again without seeing it— I care very little what the Review says except that it may help the sale—

the L. B. are exhibited in all the shops at Portsmouth but I doubt whether they have any great sale I bought one copy here *to set them going*—

I think if I was to take the trouble of puffing them off to the Commanders I could get off a few copys but I think it not worth while & therefore say nothing about them—

if they have real merit they must make their own way in the world—

29. To Dorothy Wordsworth

Address: Miss Wordsworth / Ambleside / Kendal / Westmoreland

Postmarks: PORTSMOUTH; G MAY 8 1[8]01

[Portsmouth] ⟨Tuesday⟩ Monday the 3[d] of May [1801] [1]

My dear Sister,

We have not yet sail'd the wind has been fair for this fortnight past & we have not & god knows when we shall receive our dispatches   I do not know the cause of our detention   we have had a thousand rumors about it & I am at a loss to guess the right one—   If we do not sail soon we shall lose our regular passage   I am laying here at very great expence ⟨& this is⟩   The Madras & china ships w{il}l get to China before us & spoil our Markets & this is the dullest of all dull places ⟨is . . .⟩ [2]

the Bengal fleet saild some time since & have left us behind   indeed I am out of all patience   instead of being home in 12 Months we shall be 16 or 17 or 18 Months over our voyage—   (If we do not sail in a fortnight (& we are no nearer sailing at present than we were the day we arrived) we shall most certainly loose our passage—

I am ⟨   ⟩ [3] anxious to hear from you   I hope you do not suppose that ⟨th⟩ we are half way to the Equinoctial line & on that acc^t^ have ceased writing to me—   I have got Andersons poets [4] & am at a loss where to begin   I ⟨wou⟩ should be glad if W^m^ would tell me what Poets & what Poems he thinks I *would like* most & also as far as his recollection which are the best poems—& I would be more particularly *pleased* at his pointing out any good poems in Poets such as *Logan* [5] for instance—   I have *begun* to read Shakespears works—   I cannot expres{s} how mu{ch} I have been pleased & affected with them & above all with Othello   how very differently it reads to what I remember of its acting—

⟨Wednesday.⟩ ^Tuesday^ I have this moment rec^d^ your letter with the beginning of Peter Bell—[6]   I will be much obliged to you if you would let me have as much of the poem as possible—   I do not know any thing more of St Michaels than what I have before told you   I am certain the climate would do for Col: but I doubt whether he can get any accomodation for his family—

if he goes I think *he ought first to go himself*— the voyage from Liverpool would only be about six weeks & could not prove expensive— he might have every thing for his passage settled before he left Keswick by his friends at Liverpool— I am certain the sea air alone would do him good— If he could go from W^{t}haven the better I believe the baths on the E^{t} end of the Island to be the best in the world for the Rheumatism—

I was making the corrections in the female vagrant [7] this morning when I rec^{d} your letter, I have been in daily expectation of having the corrections to the L. B by the purser but he {has not} yet arrived— I think the female va{grant very} much improved & I like ⟨the {long}⟩ the additions & corrections in the long {poem} [8] it is very beautiful & affecting—

Captn & Mrs W. left London last Saturday— they are to stay some time at York & after wards they will proceed to W^{t}haven by the way of penrith it may perhaps be some time before you see them tho I rather think as the summer is getting on that you may ‸perhaps‸ soon see them at Grasmere C[aptain] W. will be impatient to see his mother & his wifes friends at W^{t}haven to whom to he is much attach'd I am glad that you are likely to have Mary H. at Grasmere so soon [9] it will be a great relief to her for G.[allow] H.[ill] is a vile abominable place—

When you write to me at St Helena direct to ⟨Ric⟩ Staple Inn to be forwarded give my love to W^{m} & believe [me] to be your aff^{t} B. JOHN WORDSWORTH

I shall write to you once or more before we sail

30. To Mary Hutchinson

Address: Miss Hutchinson / Middleham Hall / Sedgefield / Durham [1]

Postmarks: PORTSMOUTH; G MAY 21 1801

[Portsmouth, May 19, 1801]

God bless thee my dearest Mary We are just getting under weigh with a fair Wind god grant it may continue I am in great haste

thine affectionate friend

JOHN WORDSWORTH

I did not expect we should have sail'd so early in the morning

Ship Abergany Portsmouth

May the 19th

excuse this short Note

Tuesday morning at 4 oC[l]ock

[*On another page:*] give my kindest love to Sara and George & all your Brothers *J. W*

31. To Mary Hutchinson [1]

Address: Miss Hutchinson / Gallow Hill / Wykeham / Malton

Postmark: { } 802

[11 Staple Inn, September 12, 1802] [2]

⟨My dearest Mary,⟩

I have been reading your Letter over & over again My dearest Mary till tears have come into my eyes & I known not how to express myelf thou ar't kind & dear creature But wh⟨t⟩at ever fate Befal me I shall love to the last and bear thy⟨y⟩ memory with me to the grave [3]

Thine aff[ly]

JOHN WORDSWORTH

32. To Dorothy Wordsworth

Address: Miss Wordsworth / Ambleside / Westmoreland
Postmark: A OC 22 [1]802

[11 Staple Inn, October 22, 1802]

When I ought to have rec[d] your Letter my dear Sister I was at Windsor & it was too late to answer it while you remaind at Gallow Hill,[1] I was three or 4 days at Windsor—

I was call'd from thence by my Hon'ble Masters those vile & abominable Monsters at the India House— who will finish with me by ⟨forcing⟩ making me pay 300 Guineas for my sins during the voyage— they first began about the passage through the Straits of {M}alacca.[2] & they have found they can do nothing with any of us ab[t] that. They next attack'd us with smuggling Camblets to China [3] which was alas but too true— I am to pay to 300— one Capt[n] of our fleet is fined *1,050* G[s] You must know this [is] all a new business— tho' smuggling these camblets has never been allow'd in the Service yet it has been so constantly done for years & years—by every one in ⟨the Service⟩ it—that we began to consider that we had a *right* to smuggle them— We are the first that they have fined & of cou[r]se we think it very hard & very unjust—

Capt[n] & M[rs] Wordsworth are expected in town ab[t] the beginning of November I cannot say that I like Windsor much it has too much of the *Church* about it too stiff & too formal— Mary I think is not so handsome as she was when I last saw her but she is a very fine Girl & upon the whole I was very *much* pleased with her I was disapointed a little with my aunt my Uncle is nearly the same to me ⟨allowing for his church . . .⟩ [4] making certain allowances for his profession I was a little shy with Christopher on acc[t] of his not coming to London & that My *Un*[*c*]*le* & himself *were all in all*— I might perhaps speak to him about three times when I was there [5] Geor[g]e & Mary were my companions—

Christopher is gone to Cambridge He call'd at Staple Inn ⟨upon⟩ on his passage but I saw very little of him he only stopped one day & that was I believe on account of my Uncle's being in town

I am glad & rejoyced to hear that my *Sister* Mary liked ⟨my⟩ the *choice* of *my* New Gown may she live long wear it & I see ⟨h⟩ it—

the ship is most certainly taken up whether I can ⟨come down to the⟩ ^see you^ North of England is *as yet* doubtfull I shall if possible—but the *honest* court of Directors seem'd to be inclined to give us as much trouble as possible—

The Myers's are ⟨sadly⟩ going to *Leeward* most ⟨sadly⟩ shockingly every one speaks against them & it is thought ^& most cer⟨tain⟩^ that Tom Myers will loose his election [6] I have seen M[rs] Robinson she laments the folly of Myers & I thought spoke with a great *deal of good sense* & *impartiality* both of the Election & his marriage— [7] Myers himself could not have stated the circumstance more favourably for his own cause than *she* did to Rich[d] and myself—

I have not seen Charles Lamb since you left town I

have made many pious reso[l]utions of calling upon him but have allways broken them—

I am going with Rich[d] tomorrow morning to Windsor we only stay over Sunday— We have got horses & shall have pleasant rides by Richmond & Hampton Court if the Weather be fine but [at] present it is inclined to be Rainy—

Give my kindest love to Mary and W[m] and I am
Your Affectionate Brother
JOHN WORDSWORTH

33. To Dorothy Wordsworth

Address: Miss Wordsworth / Ambleside / Westmoreland
Postmark: A NO 8 [1]802

[11] Staple Inn Nov[r] 7th *Sunday* [1802]

My dear Sister,

I am exceedingly sorry to hear you have been so unwell [1] indeed your account of yourself wase more *shamefull* than my own tho we were upon diferent *tacks* *I* have the advantage of you for you must know I have bought a *horse & a Gig* [2] I drive all about London I can scarse tell you where I have *not* been Windsor is *nothing to me* in distance I am even going to see Christopher at Cambridge but to tell you the truth I never had such good health in London as I have at present this is on acc[t] of the *country air* which I have the *pleasure* of enjoying— I shall send W[m] ⟨the⟩ Anderson's Poets I only whish for Spenser out of the whole colection but that I shay [*for* shall] buy in London tell W[m] I wish he would let me know what books he thinks would suit me best to the amount of 20. or 30£ to take to sea with me—[3] I ⟨ ⟩[4] do not kown what I should like myself Shakespear is the only man I like at present & yet one cannot for a voyage of 16 months constantly *stick* to him—

The Morning Post ⟨I constantly⟩ on acc^t^ of Coleridge you may be assured I constantly look after Yesterday ⟨ ⟩[5] his Letter to Mr Fox[6] appear'd I wanted to buy the paper in the City & afterwards at the Morning post office but I could not get it ⟨th⟩ I have seen the Letter & have one objection to make that I think no man who ⟨publickly ad⟩ in a publick *manner* makes an address to another ought to shew any marks of humiliation— independence is the order of the day—and a very good order too— I have been to the Play to see Mr Reynolds' new Comedy of Delays and Blunders[7] it is the most farcical tragical funny thing I ever saw in my life I do not ⟨think⟩ that any thing would succeed upon the stage but vulgar low tricks in comedy & rant in Tragedy I have seen Rich^d^ the 3^d^ by Cook[8] but except the name of the play it is no more like what Shakespear has written than Jack the Giant Killer— I do not like Cook in Richard

I am sorry to hear that poor Sara has been so unwell

I wish I could see her at Grasmere—or I wish I could see her and Grasmere at the same time— I have not seen Mr Russell nor do I think I can see [him] before this Letter is sent off I wish to call upon the Lamb's on Acc^t^ of *Miss Lamb* but I have put it off till I am quite ashamed— I have seen *your Acct* of W^m's^ marriage[9] in the morning post it is not quite so bad as I thought it would have been from what you said— I had heard of it before from my Uncle at Windsor—which made me whish to see it the Children were pleased with the playthings the Poem neither My Uncle or *Christopher* could understand so of course it went for nothing the

⟨p . . .⟩ [10] Drawings were after *due* deliberation pronounced to be excellent   as for Mary you would not expect her to say or *feel* any things different from her father & Mother   I am under the disagreeable necessity of being obliged to pay a visit to Windsor with ⟨John⟩ Tom Myers and young Cooper   I have wishd to get off the conection but I do not think ⟨that⟩ I can—   they *stick* too close to me.—   My Aunt wishes to see Cooper ⟨ ⟩ [11] & I should like to go with him but I do not like Myers & more particularly after what I have said to my Uncle W^m^ of him—   Rich^d^ is well very busy being *term* time   we ride out together very regularly—   I have just return'd with him from a most pleasant ride in the country   *we can afford it*— [12]

I am Your Affectionate Brother JOHN WORDSWORTH

There is a reward of 50£ offer'd for apprehendind the infamous Col. Hope [13]   I do not understand that part of the ⟨peom that says there is something in this *persons* ⟨char⟩ history ⟨that⟩ (I mean Mary.) ⟩ [14]

I have seen Colridge [15]   he will write tomorrow

Give my kind love to my Brother & Sister

JW—

34. To Dorothy Wordsworth

Address: Miss Wordsworth / Ambleside / Westmoreland / Single

Postmark: A DE 2 [1]802

[11 Staple Inn,]

Wednesday 1st [and Thursday 2] Dec^br^ [1802]

My dear Sister,

I am sorry to find that you have not yet got the better

of *this* most violent illness [1] indeed it is a great shame & I insist upon it that you get well as soon as possible You will be pleased to hear that Rich^{d} has been with Mr Graham [2] who has just arrived in town and Mr G. tells him that our acc^{ts} with Lord Lonsdale will be duly *truly* & *honourably* &c: settled about Christmas that the said L^{d} L has not got money wherewithall to pay the whole of the sum owing ^⟨to . . .⟩ [3]^ to us ⟨at Christmas⟩ on acc^{t} of the great demands upon the estate but that security will be given for the ⟨y⟩ payment of the whole & that part perhaps two three or four thousand pounds will be paid at Christmas— Mr Graham was very kind to Rich^{d} & seem'd to be much intrested for us ⟨he said . . . that there was no doubt of . . . ^⟨the whole of⟩^ the money—⟩

Lord Lowther has been most uncommonly attentive to Captn & Mrs Wordsworth they were of the first party invited to Lowther Hall— just before they came to London Lord Lowther call'd upon them & treated them with most *distinguished respect*

I have the pleasure to inform you that Mr Myers will most certainly be kick'd out of Parliament every thing goes agai[n]st him at Harwich & Mr Robinson Wordsworth [4] has been making such a fool of himself that I should not be much surprized if he should follow him—*out of his situation* Capt. W. who of course felt intrested that his brother out of prudence alone should vote with Mr R. went down to Harwich with a wish to get him to support Mr R. but he has gone obstinately against him—

when Capt. W ⟨ask^{d}⟩ call'd at his house he never asked him to sit down told him he had never been of any service to him (the Captn has lent him upwards of 1.000.£) & that the Myers' were his great friends—

Colridge left London unexpectedly [5] I did not see

so much of him as I aught it happen'd most unfortunately that we were *both* much engaged ⟨&⟩ he looks I think poorly he does not seem to have the life and spirits that he used to have—& yet he was *very* entertaining I should be glad to hear where he is gone & what he is doing it is a sad thing that M[r] Wedgewood should be so *most unfortunatly* ill— as I *seldom* write of course I could not think of asking him to write to me—

I have just rec[d] your Letter from S[t] Helena *it came by the* last ships for which as in duty ⟨bound⟩ and love bound I must thank you I think I'll have it seal'd up and sent to me for the next voyage

Indeed my dear Sister I cannot express the pleasure I should feel at seeing your { }[6] I am with you constantly & { }[7] dearly

Your Affec[t] Broth{er}
JOHN WORDSWORTH

Tuesday [*for* Thursday] 2[d] Copy of a Letter sent to Lowther by Rich[d] Sir, Having been desired by M[r] James Graham to make out a correct acc[t] of my fathers demand upon the late Earl of Londsdale, I take the liberty to transmit to you such acc[t] on the other half sheet with the particulars of the Law charges and expence incurred by my fathers representatives in and about establishing the demand— I beg leave to repeat that I shall at all times with the utmost readiness give every explanation of the acct[s] in my power that may be required— I request that you will represent to Lord Lowther that I am authorized by my brothers & sister to say that we are willing to refer these matters to any Gentleman his Lordship will please to name but I trust there are no solid objection to the acc[ts] as I have as yet heard of no specific objection. However should there be any I will endeavour to answer them without delay, it being my most ardent desire to avoid any unnecessary expence & to give as little trouble to Ld Lowther & his friends as possible   I am Sir—&c

To John Richardson Esqr Lowther hall
the Estate of the E^{l} of Londsdale deceased to John W. deceased   D^{r} [8]

To balance of general cash acc^{t} at the time of Mr John W. decease deliver'd—	1192. 14. 9¾		
To amount of Law charges at the same time Deliverd—	3432. 8. 10		4625. 3. 7¾
	Intrest on D°		4336. 1. 10
			8961. 5. 10 [9]
To amount of Mr Rich Wordsworths bill for Law charges deliver'd 20th of May 1794—	972. 13. 7		
To intrest on D° from the 20th May 1795 to 20 Septr 1802 being 7 years and 4 months	259. 7. 7		1232. 1. 2
To the amount of expence paid various witnesses not included in M^{r} W bill of costs—			195.
It ends as true Law bill ought to do.[10]			£10. 388. 6. 8

Ric^{d} desires me to say that it is possible the money may not be paid at Christmas it may be two or three months afterwards and also that the sum at first paid may perhaps not exceed 1.500£. but L[d] Lowther has refer'd the business to M[r] Graham & M[r] G. will endeavour to settle it as soon as possible   the demands upon L[d] L are upwards of 200.000£.—

35. To Dorothy Wordsworth

Address: Miss Wordsworth / Ambleside / Westmoreland
Postmark: A DE 17 [1]802

[11 Staple Inn, December 17, 1802][1]

My dear Sister,

I have this moment rec[d] your Letter & I have this moment returnd from Windsor.   the children have been exceedingly ill in but are now better   I am so ⟨shaken⟩ stiff & shaken with my ride that I do not know what to do with my own *head*   they have been ⟨avoi⟩ deserted by friends neighbours & I had almost said relations till I made my appearance   even the newspaper⟨s⟩ ^from my Uncles'^ was not allow'd to shew it self in the houses of the worthy cannons[2] for fear of contagion—

⟨They are quite⟩   the children are now *quite* well   I do not believe they were ever in *great* danger but I suppose it is natural for *parents* to be alarmed—

I have got your *Gowns* &[c.] from Miss Lambs but when you will have them I cannot tell   In the first [place] they shall not go by sea—

The Ship ^viz the E[l] of Aberg[y] [3]^ is to be survey'd tomorrow & I am obliged to take myself off to ⟨by⟩ Gravesend so that I cannot see the box packed up nor can I have time to get *Rich[d]* & my clothes packed up   therefore you must wait & with patience too   I shall not buy the Dictionary but will send the Andersons Poets with your parcels for sara.   she is so naughty in being ill that I am quite ashamed of her for a sister—[4]   I am much pleased with W^ms sonnet to Bonaparte [5] I think it is well written—[6] it is like the rest of his sonnets which I have seen not much likely to please *common* people at the first sight but I think they are very good—yet still I think it is a pity he should employ himself in that way

My China shoes are all on b^d of ship but if there are any in town they shall be sent— I have the pleasure to inform you that tea and all my articles ⟨are⟩ of private trade have risen a great deal as much perhaps as two thousand pound upon the whole of my investment—since you were in town

Lord Lowthers business is the same I have written this in great haste as I do not know ⟨as I am⟩ ^being^ obliged to go down to the ship tomorrow when I shall have an opportunity of writing to you— give my kindest Love to my sister Mary Sara & W^m

Yours aff^y JOHN WORDSWORTH—

You may be sorry for John Myers but I hate him I do not think there is much real goodness about him he thinks he has served me & I believe he has *too* but I do not like the principal upon which it *has & was* done— but I must say that I am still & always have been upon good terms with him—

36. To Samuel Taylor Coleridge

Source: Collected Letters of Samuel Taylor Coleridge, ed. Earl Leslie Griggs, II (Oxford, 1956), 921 (No. 487, to Thomas Wedgwood, February 10, 1803)

. . . . .

Mr Wedgewood shall have the pictures [1] if we return

to bring them home. Indeed, I should find the greatest pleasure in serving or pleasing him in any thing. But I hope, I shall be able to get some for him before we sail. The Bang [2] if possible shall also be sent: if any country Ship [3] arrives, I shall certainly get it. We have not got any thing of the Kind in our China Ships.

. . . . .

37. To William Wordsworth

Text: Postscript of letter from RW to WW, February 14, 1803 (DCP)

[11 Staple Inn, February 14, 1803]

My dear Brother, I am happy to inform you that our affairs with Ld Lowther are likely soon to be settled to the satisfaction ^I hope^ of both parties but Rich^{d} will give you better information than I can possibly do I shall write to you tomorrow I have a great deal to say about my own concerns

I am Yours Affec^{t} JOHN WORDSWORTH

38. To Dorothy Wordsworth

Address: Miss Dorothy Wordsworth / Ambleside / Westmorland [1]

Postmark: A FE 21 [1]803

[11 Staple Inn, February 21, 1803] [2]

My dear Sister, I have rec^{d} your last Letter and intended to write to W^{m} but I hope it will be the same

thing if what I am going to say is *addressed* to you—
I was yesterday with Mr James Graham & he has promised to pay immediately three thousand pounds on our acc^t in consequence of my *speedy* departure to India this was intended by him to serve me— now you must know that as the times are at present I can not take any *Goods* out in private trade on acc^t of our last bad markets and that it will be a very great *object* to me to have as much money as possible ⟨ ⟩[3] in dollars—for by dollars I am sure of gaining at least twenty per Cent. without any risk and have a better chance of buying my teas in the country—[4] I shall this voyage make very well out of my homeward bound investment but I lost very much *outward*—which can not be the case if I take dollars—

any Security you may want with respect to that part of the money I shall take out, Rich^d will be ready to give— I have also one thing more to say that Mr Robinsons share of the Abergany will shortly be sold— & it is recommended that *we* should purchase it—[5] it is of great consequence that it should be bought both to Captn Wordsworth & myself but rest assured I should never wish you ⟨ ⟩[6] W^m to have any share in it till I am satisfied that it will give you good intrest for your money— and of that I shall take care that Rich^d shall have good information before (⟨it⟩ if you should approve of it) it is bought—

I supose that it may sell for 2,000 pounds—which will be about 400£ apiece— I have consulted with some men of known experience in these things & they say it is worth 2.500£ & 2.700, to me— If it does not give you clear 5 or 6 per cent I would not wish you to have any share of the ship—

I would thank you to let me hear from you immediately   I have been sworn in & am in hopes we shall sail in less than six weeks   I am anxious to get off as soon as possible for {I} think it is of great consequence —to be here in one of the first of the large ships for I may then with the *assistance* of my friends *hope* to get a better voyage—   I wish W^m^ would by all means see Captn W. when he comes down into the North and *insist* upon my having a better voyage this next season

I have had a letter from Coleridge who wishes to go a voyage with me to China & I do not [know] what to say about it   I think it would do him good but I think it [would] be better if he would go to Italy but still he seems bent upon going for I have had *two* letters from him   I shall consult with my friends & if he *really* wishes to go & I *can* take him (for the Comp^s^ orders are agai[n]st it) I shall with great pleasure—but I think I shall be blamed for taking him from his Wife and family   I am going down to the ship early tomorrow for she is coming out of dock—   give my kind & most affectionate love to Mary & W^m^ & Sara

& I am Your Aff. b^r^ JOHN WORDSWORTH

39. To William Wordsworth

Address: Mr Wordsworth / Ambleside / Westmorland / Single Sheet
Postmark: C AP 16 [1]803

[11] Staple Inn April 16th [1803]

My dear W^m^

Rich^d^ has rec^d^ & I have seen the Letter which you last wrote to him about Lord Lowthers debt which is still remaining due to us & also of the three thousand pounds which Rich[d] has already received—[1]

Now for myself I must say that it is absolutely necessary that I should have the whole of the three thousand pounds or I had better resign the command of the ship for if I have not money it is not possible that I make money & it happens unfortunatly that most of the goods which we take out to China require ready money for the purchace of them— I have got the command of the ship under such favourable circumstances that if any money is to be made in the Service I must make it— With respect to the security I certainly can never ask Rich[d] to become ⟨ ⟩[2] security for all my debts—& for this reason that I already owe him two thousand pounds & 1.500 to Capt[n] Wordsworth—which they have lent me on ⟨their⟩ ^my^ own security alone—

My request of you is this that as most likely we shall receive 5. or 6. thousand pounds in addition to the 3.000 pounds already received that the whole of my share may be consider'd to be already pay'd; which ^share^ may amount to 1.800 £ & there will then remain 1.200 £ ⟨which I shall owe to to⟩ of which 1.200 £ your share will be 300 £. now I ask you to lend me this three hundred pound upon my own security—[3] I am not asking you for the whole of your property for god knows that if the whole sum which Lord L. owes us was paid & you were to offer me the whole of it I would not take it because I know there is a risque—every person who is concerned in trade must have a risque—but it does not follow that ⟨the⟩ it is to extend to the whole amount of the property— ⟨because I am insured.⟩ I expect to leave Gravesend about Saturday & I hope we may be in the Downs by this day fortnight—

I am much obliged to you for the poems which M[r] Cook brought me[4] I like the Cuckow the Sparrows Nest the Butterfly the Celandine the first part of the leech gatherer very much indeed & particularly the Cuckow— the other poems I do not like so well as the Lyrical Ballads—

I wish I may get the other poems which you have promised me— Rich[d] is out & I ⟨shall leave the rest of the⟩ and as he may have something to say ab[t] L. Lowthers affairs I shall leave [the] ⟨remainder⟩ ^rest^ of the sheet for him Give my Kindest Love to Mary & Dorothy

I am Your Aff[te]

JOHN WORDSW[*flourish*]

P [S] It is uncertain whether Rich[d] will be in before the post goes out

40. To Captain John Wordsworth

Address: Capt Wordsworth / Brougham Hall / Penrith / Cumberland / Single

Postmark: C AU 9 1804

Ship Earl of Abergavenny [August 8, 1804]

My dear Cousin,

I have the pleasure to inform you that the Abergãny is arrived safe in the Channel under convoy of his Majestys ship the Plantagenet of 74 Guns and in Company with the whole of the China fleet sixteen in number including ourselves— We arrived in China on the 3 of Sep[tr] (1803) having made a very quick passage and by that means excaped the violent tufoon in the China Seas in which the Coutts was dismasted and most of the ships that sail'd with and some before us (viz the Hope & Dorsetshire 10 Days) suffer'd very much. The Supercargoes detained us five months in China expecting convoy or to hear from England by the Woodford she was upwards of eight months over her passage and when she arrived the Coutts and all the ships of the Fleet being ready to sail we were dispatched without Convoy and with the country ships under our charge on the 6th of Febr 1804 leaving the Woodford in China— Our orders were to proceed through the Straits of Malacca & we went to the Westward of the Paraceles and Pulo Sapater and to the Eastward of Pulo Auro we fell in with Admiral Lenios and his Squadron (and our success against him I am happy that you have heard) [1] he had been waiting *to take* us for some months & had modestly reserved for his share only seven of us the rest were to be taken by three Frigates and a Brig he had with him this news we heard at Malacca and they were so much apprehensive for our safety that they saluted the Commodore with 21 Guns upon our arrival.— I am happy to add that we have met with no accidents, gales of Wind &c: &c no damage of any description & that the ship has suffer'd as little as if she had ⟨been⟩ remain'd in Mr Pitchers dock for the time she has been out— I return you my sincere thanks for the very kind Letter I received ⟨dated⟩ at St Helena dated (Brougham Hall Christmas Eve 1803) and congratulate you upon your military appointment [2] You seem to be so well prepared to meet ⟨the great⟩ Bonaparte the great Emperor of the Gauls [3] that he will ⟨know better⟩ never attempt to land his troops in England and I cannot help admiring the courage and spirit of the Country— I am also glad to find that Mr Pitt is first Minister—

Mr Stewart[4] will give you an account and I am (concerned to say) a bad one of Ponqua's affairs[5] and the prospect you have of (only) getting the principal of the money from him: Mr Drummond inform'd me that two years intrest would be paid on that part of his debt which was contracted ⟨before⟩ about the time and before yours. I fear that he owes Mr Drummond a great deal of money which keeps *him* in China but this will certainly be the means of settling your accounts sooner as Mr D. has taken upon himself to settle the whole of ⟨them.—⟩ Ponqua's affairs himself or at least to put them in such a train as they will speedily be settled—

We have just pass'd Dungeness light house and I have ⟨just⟩ ^only^ time to say that we are all well Joseph tells me he has written to you give my best Love to Mrs Wordsworth & I am your affectionate

Cousin

JOHN WORDSWORTH

Ship Abergãny
Aug^st 8th 1804

41. To Captain John Wordsworth

Address: Captn John Wordsworth / Brougham Hall / Penrith / Cumberland

Postmark: B AU 16 [1]804

[11] Staple Inn Aug^st 15th 1804.

My dear Cousin,

I had the pleasure of receiving your Letter this morning written at the end of my Brothers when I wrote to you I did not give you any account of my outward bound investment for as I neither did well or ill with it I wishd to hear how my teas were likely to sell for on that part of my investment the whole success of my voyage must depend. Opium and Quicksilver were the only things in the China market that sold to any profit.

My teas are principally low priced black and green teas and I am told I shall do very well with them but the *utmost* that I can now expect is ⟨to⟩ ^that they will^ make up for the great loss which I sustained last voyage—

I was with Mr Dent [1] this morning and spoke to him of the *necessity* of my having a better than a China direct voyage [2] I ⟨him⟩ told the losses which I had suffer'd last voyage and the little probability of making any thing by this—and I am sure he felt very much for my situation I read to him that part of your letter in which you had intrested yourself with so much kindness with Mr Wallace [3] to get me a Bombay and China voyage and he seem'd very much pleased with it he particularly recommended to me to write to you to request that you would give me a letter of introduction to Mr Wallace for he wishes me to state my situation to him & thinks that Mr Wallace *might* be induced to exert himself *still more* on my behalf ^If I was to wait upon him myself.) ^ Mr Dent then told me that he had spoken to Sir Francis Baring [4] & would go immediately to Mr Lushinton [5] and whatever he could do for me I might depend upon should be done— He has also invited me to his house to stay with [him] as often and as long as I like & indeed has far exceeded in his expressions to serve me my utmost expectation You will see by todays papers the flattering mention that is made of the China fleet— I can assure you it gives me very little pleasure compared to the solid advantage that I might obtain by ^procuring^ a

Bombay & China voyage *could I get one*— I am sorry that Mr Stewarts Letter has miscarried I told him of it to day & he will write to you again I had a most kind letter from my Uncle W^m^ this morning & am sorry to hear by it that he has lost one of [his] children since we sail'd—[6] he wishes very much to see me in Norfolk.—

We have two pipes of Madeira Wine[7] in the ship & you may have one or both if you think proper I have not tasted the Wine but believe it to be good it was bought upon a private trade speculation— I have also brought Mrs Wordsworth some tea which I shall send down as soon as possible & if I ⟨have any⟩ there is anything in the ship that I thought would be acceptable I should be very glad— I was pleased to hear that Mrs Wordsworth was well & my Aunt improved in her health I am afraid to ask after old nurse but if she be well remmember me to her and Mary for I *conclude* that she is with you still— We had a very bad and tedious passage up the river[8] & split more sails than we have done the whole voyage the Ganges carried away her topmasts in one of the Squalls. I did not arrive in Staple Inn till last night & was much disappointed to hear that Rich^d^ was out of town ⟨but⟩ I have no doubt he has been spending a pleasant time among his friends in Cumberland & I was sati[s]fied in ⟨hearing⟩ ^having heard^ from almost all my friends that I was anxious to hear of.

Give my kindest love to Mrs Wordsworth & I am Your

Affectionate Cousin

JOHN WORDSWORTH

I have not written to my Brother for I do not know where a Letter will reach him—

J. W

42. To Captain John Wordsworth

Address: {Ca}pt^{n} John Wordsworth / Brougham Hall / Penrith / Cumberland [1]

Receiving House stamp: { }t Stre{et} / { }nsd{ }

[11] Staple Inn Augst 22^{d} 1804

My dear Cousin,

I received my Brothers Letter this morning and immediately waited upon Mr Dent who had just received yours I cannot help saying I was very much hurt when I found so little was likely to be got from Mr Wallace Mr Dent carried me to the India House where he saw Mr Grant the deputy Chairman and Mr Grant told him that Mr Wallace had never spoken to him on the subject—and Mr Dent and myself are both of [the] opinion that he has never spoken to the Chairman—

I have represented my affairs to Mr Dent so strongly that I am certain that he will do all in his power to serve me but I am afraid his applications will be too late— I have given up all thoughts of a Bombay and China voyage but shall be most greviously disapointed if I do not get a better than a China direct one I am going to write this evening to Lord Aberg̃any [2] Mr Percival has kindly undertaken to deliver the letter for me, I do not expect much from him & yet I would leave nothing undone which might have been done I have applied wherever I have thought there was a proba[bi]lity of Success and can hope little except from Mr Dent—
Do you think you could do me any good by writing to Lord Abergany?— I am sorry that I should give you so much trouble only you will see that this is a matter of so much consequence that I am sure you will excuse it— I had a letter from my Brother Christopher this

morning who tells me he has got a living in Norfolk given him by the Bishop of 400 £ a year—

Give my Kind Love to M[rs] Wordsworth
& I am Yours Aff[ly]
JOHN WORDSWORTH [3]

43. To Captain John Wordsworth

Address: Capt[n] Wordsworth / Brougham Hall / Penrith / Cumberland / *In another hand:* Grassmere
Postmark: A SE 15 [1]804

Staple Inn N° 11 Sept 15th 1804

My dear Cousin,

I have the pleasure to inform you that I have at last succeeded in getting a voyage far beyond my expectation I could almost say my wishes— the nomination has been given to M[r] Dent by Sir Francis Baring it is the fifth there will be three or 4 Bombay and China ship[s] 1 large Bengal and China 1 D° Madras 1 Bencoolen & China so that I shall have the choice most likely of Bengal. Madras. & S[t] Helena & Bencoolen I shall not hesitate in choosing Bengal which I am told will do exceeding well— the ships will be taken up on Wednesday next—when I shall write and give you a full account of my prospects &c— I cannot express the trouble and anxiety I have had upon this occasion I have been ill and well, well and ill according as my hopes have been raisd or depressed but however it has been of this service to me that I have found and made friends that are very powerful and very willing to serve me—
In the first place I must inform you that I have almost

^a^ certain ⟨hopes⟩ prospect of getting for my next voyage a Bombay and China voyage thro' Mr Grant who will be Chairman next year Mr Wilberforce[1] is my great friend there and had I applied to him sooner I should have had a Bombay and China voyage on Mr Grant's the Deputy's nomination— Mr Dent desired his compt^{s} to you and begged me to say that ⟨he had not⟩ the reason he did not answer your Letter was that he could give you no hopes of success— you will most likely see him in the north of England in less than a months time— Mr Harris I have got out as Chief Mate of a Bombay & China ship Baggott will be first again Stewart second and Joseph third My Uncle Cookson who has been presented to a very valuable living by the King has been of great service to me introducing me to the Thortons,[2] Wilberforce, Twinings[3] &c the Bodingtons he has been in town some time he left it yesterday but will return again on Tuesday—

Give my kindest love to Mrs Wordsworth & to my Aunt and Mrs Barker I am Dear Cousin yours &c

JOHN WORDSWORTH

44. To Dorothy Wordsworth

Address: { } Westmor{land}
Postmark: Missing

Staple Inn N° 11
Septr 15th 1804

My dear Sister,

I have the pleasure to inform you that I have at last succeded in getting a voyage far beyond my expectation

I had almost said my wishes the nomination has been given to Mr Dent by Sir Francis Baring it is the fifth and as there will be four Bombay and China Ships I shall have the choice of going to Bengal Madras or St Helena Bencoolen & China— I shall not hesitate in choosing Bengal and I am told I shall do exceeding well— the ships will be taken up on Wednesday next to prevent any further applications for voyages to the Court of directors—

I cannot express the trouble and anxiety I have had upon this occasion I have been ill and well well and ill according as my hopes have been rais'd or depressd however it has been of this service to me that I have found and made friends that are both very powerful and very willing to assist me— I have almost a certain prospect of getting for my next voyage a Bombay and China voyage thro' Mr Wilberforce who is the great friend & Brother labourer in the same vineyard [1] with Mr Grant the Chairman of the Court of directors—

had he been applied to about 4 months sooner I might have had a Bombay & China voyage— Mr Dent has been exceeding kind to me—

Mr Sharp ha{ } [2] through the Bodingtons { } good & I am much { } time had so far { } to despair of Mr { } Mr S. speaks highly { } as a most fine a { } congratul[at]e you u{pon } little girl [3]—{ } able to see yo{u } affairs will detain{ } I do not think I can { } leave London I recd{ } and the nomina{tion } night

Sarah H{utchinson } [4]
Dorothy W{ordsworth }

45. To Captain John Wordsworth

Address: Capt[n] Wordsworth / Brougham Hall / Penrith / Cumberland / Single
Postmark: B O[C] 13 [1]80[4]

[11] Staple Inn Oct[r] 12th 1804

My dear Cousin,

I wrote you some time since a very long Letter which I am sorry to hear from my Brother Rich'd has miscarried I rec[d] Rich[ds] Letter on Wednesday and should have written to you immediately but have had ten hours attendance at the India House for two days in consequence of the Arrival of the Bengal Fleet the Directors were so ⟨bus⟩ much employ'd in reading the Dispatches that they could not white wash us [1] and swear us in this has at last been accomplishd as you will see by todays papers—

I am much obliged to you for both your Letters which I rec[d] & I shall now endeavour to give you the best account of myself that I can—

You will see that my voyage is changed from Bombay to Bengal [2] & I ⟨must inform you as well as I can how it took place⟩ Hamilton of the Bombay Castle had the Chairmans nomination and without consulting him the Chairman appointed ⟨him to the⟩ ^the Ship to a^ Bengal voyage wishing to surprize him with something that the Chairman thought would be beyond Hamiltons expectations— as the voyage was new and given out by some at that time as a voyage of speculation Hamilton wishd to have a Bombay nomination and applied to the Chairman for that purpose and the Chairman and Sir Francis Baring agreed to exchange & I am happy to add with M[r] Dents approbation— ⟨When⟩

^Some time after^ the voyage was exchanged the Chairman sent for me and told me (I never was introduced to him by any person) that he congratulated me on having got what he conce[i]ved to be the best voyage in the Service he told me that I should have ⟨a great m a⟩ every advantage that the Bombay Ships had and the probability of a great many more— he said that he had rec^{d} a Letter from Captn Craig of the Elphinstone who told him that the pilots in the River assured him that they would as soon take charge of that ship as any eight hundred ton ship in the Service [3] and he gave orders for me to have whatever Journals I thought proper from the India house and told me he would be glad to give me every information ⟨I h⟩ that I might think necessary— ⟨I have⟩ he has sent for me several times since I first saw him and offerd to send letters overland or to afford me any assistance in that or any other way in his power— I have the greatest confidence that this voyage will turn out something very good if not very great

in the first place there is no doubt but that I shall have a *whole cargo* of passengers to Bengal [4] and I am happy to ⟨add that⟩ say from the acc^{ts} rec^{d} by these last arrivals a certainty of doing well with my outward bound investment— these ships have sold for fifty per Cent all round none less than forty or forty five ⟨and no Ships have⟩ there is no doubt but that I shall get as much cotton ⟨of⟩ ^upon^ freight as I like to take in and upon better terms than at Bombay—& with the probability of taking on my own acc^{t} three times as much as the Bombay capt^{s}. I shall also ⟨a⟩ ^have^ chance of making by opium [5] and Rice &c. &c. and I think I may have passengers home— These advantages I am certain you will think superior to a Bombay voyage and as I have been in Bengal [6] I do not think the dangers of the River [7] so great as is generally represented—and this is the opinion of Mr Woolmore the Chairman any [*for* and] many persons—

The officers will all be examined and sworn in today

I was down at the Survey of the ship on tuesday last ⟨and⟩ nothing is wanting to be done to the Ship and she will be out of dock by this day week she has deliverd an excellent cargo & I believe is altogether in very good order as we are to be afloat on the 22 Ins^t you cannot expect that either Joseph or myself can with any propriety have the pleasure of seeing you in Cumberland indeed my letter which miscarried would have explained that sufficiently—

I am sorry to inform you that Speeke has behaved so ill upon this last voyage that it would be impossible for me to take him out again & particularly upon this voyage when we are likely to have passengers he was constan[t]ly drunk ⟨during the voyage⟩ and took so little care of my stores that I was obliged to act as steward myself I believe he is going to set off for the West Indies but cannot tell as he never ⟨was⟩ ^has been^ near me except once since we arrived in England and that was to make a demand of money which I had paid once and some part of the Bill twice— I believe he owes you money and if any part of it could be secured it would be proper I wish your directions upon this matter—

he is himself so conscious of his bad behaviour that I am certain he never will apply to me to take him again— Akers is an exceeding good steady man but I am sorry to say has suffer'd so much from the Liver complaint that I would not recomend him to take another voyage Thorp the Carpenter had also a very severe attack of the Liver I have often dined with Mr Crawshay [8] he is going to let me have as much Iron and Steel as I like upon my own terms, and he intends to prevail upon his Father who is daily expected in town to lend me two Thousand pounds— I dined with my cousin Ann [9] and Mr Favell [10] at Mr Crawshays she looks very well and was in great Spirits—

I cannot get the Wine out of the India house till Mr Dent arrives in Town I am glad you have disposed of one of the pipes to Lord Lowther & I wish you would take the other to yourself give my kind Love to Mrs Wordsworth & tell her that I am much obliged to her for her kind remembrance of me I have bought in some tea & a handsome deserts set of China & some other things the particulars of which I shall write to her as soon as possible With my kind love to My Aunt and Mrs Barker

I am Your Affectionate
Cousin J. WORDSWORTH

46. To Captain John Wordsworth

Address: Captn Wordsworth / Messrs Wilkinson & Crosthwaite / Fenchurch Street / No 8 / London
Postmark: PORTSMOUTH 7⟨3⟩

[Portsmouth, January 23, 1805]

My dear Cousin,

We have arrived at Portsmouth after a most extra[o]rdinary piece of good luck in escaping from the Warren Hastings in the Downs which ship drifted on board of us in a very heavy gale of wind from the W^t^Ward— I can not express how happy I am that she has done us so little damage she struck us on the starboard bow and carried away [1] the Cathead and Anchor Stock [2] and then rebounded from the ship and drifted past us—with out any other damage— she has received much hurt they say two thousand pounds will not repair it and most likely will be left at Portsmouth for the next convoy—[3]

her stern frame is not damaged but her Gun & poop decks are compleately torn up— had she touch'd our Bowsprit it must have gone with the same blow and our three Masts— I can not say how glad I am we have escaped so well, most of the ships lost both anchors and cables & I think we have suffer'd as little in point of expence of damage as any of them— Mr Evans & his family [4] are down and I hope as the Wind continues from the Eastward we shall see Mr Stewart very soon [5] Mr Evans says he will be dispatched tomorrow. We have had a very hard passage of it from Gravesend myself and every person on board much exposed to the cold and I am ⟨myself⟩ at present not very well we had a very bad night of it the night we came round to Portsmouth nothing but snow and Sleet—

I hope to hear tomorrow that the troops are on their way to the ship & that they will embark in the Evening or early the next day I am sorry that we are to have such a large proportion of Compn^ys^ [6] they say upwards of a hundred and twenty and about 30 or 40 Kings—[7]

Major Ottway the Kings Com^g^ Officer I am told is a very pleasant man and I think considering the number of passengers that we shall do very well—

The post is going out & I have just time to beg that

you will remember [me] most Affecly to Mrs Wordsworth & wish my Compliments to the Family in Fenchurch S^{t}

I am Dear Cousin in haste
Yours Most Sincerely
JOHN WORDSWORTH

Portsmouth Jany 23^{d} 1804 [*for* 1805]

I will write to you again as soon as possible I have had a great many letters to write to the passengers and many who are down have engaged my attention [a] great part of this day and the ships concerns alike I have orderd a new Cable

47. To William Wordsworth

Address: Wm Wordsworth Esqr / Ambleside / Westmorland

Postmark: PORTSMOUTH 73

Ship Abergavenny
at Portsmouth Jany 24th [1805]

My dear W^{m}

I ought to have written to you long ago but I have a most utter dislike to writing if I can avoid it, and I can assure you tho no man of business myself I have had quite enough to engage the attention of a man more fitted for it than myself— I have the pleasure to inform you that the Abergany is arrived safe at Portsmouth and if the Wind continues fair which it is at present I shall expect to leave this place tomorrow We had a very narrow escape in the Downs the Warren Hastings Indiaman ⟨ran⟩ $_{\wedge}$drifted$_{\wedge}$ foul of us and in a heavy gale of wind but fortunately did us little damage, she has sufferd so much that ⟨she⟩ ^we^ are order'd to proceed to sea without her.— The Purser is dispatched & I expect him at Portsmouth every hour the Convoy appointed is the Weymouth Frigate of 44 Guns— I have been so much engaged since I arrived in england that I regret very much it has been out of my power to pay yoŭ a visit in the North of England and I can assure [you] that except to ⟨the shi visit⟩ ^see^ the Ship I have not been three times out of London since we arrived

My Investment is well laid in & my voyage thought by most persons the first of the season and if we are so fortunate as to get safe and soon to Bengall I mean before any other ship of the season I have no doubt but that I shall make a very good voyage of it if not a *very great* one—at least this is the general opinion— I have ⟨been⟩ got my investment upon the best of terms having paid ready money ⟨for it⟩ ^great part of it^ which I was enabled to do by one Gentlemans lending me 5.000 £— ⟨my investment⟩ it ammounts to about 20.000 £—in goods and money—

The passenger[s] are all down and we are anxiously expecting to sail we shall muster at my table 36 or 38 persons [1] this must alone have given me a great deal of trouble to procure provisions &c for them [2] ⟨&c⟩ & I was obliged to apply to the Court of Director[s] to have some of the passagers turn'd out of the Ship which was granted I thought at one time I should have had 45 persons at my table—

In Ships Company we have 200 [3] and Soldiers and passengers 200 more amounting altogether to 400 so that I shall have sufficient employment on my hands to keep all these people in order—

I should have liked very much to have seen the poetry

you have written (which I have not seen)— in the Lyrical Ballads my favorites are the Mad mother part of the Indian Woman and Joanna— I like Michael and all the poems on the naming of places but Joanna best— and I also like { }n [4] The poem of the wye is a poem that I admire but after having read it I do not like to turn to it again— among those unpublis'd that I have seen my favorite is the Leach gather[er] the Sparrows Nest and Butterfly and Cuckow— there is a harshness in many of the others which I do not like— I think the Lyrical Ballad[s] taken alltoge[the]r far superior to the last poems—

Remember me most affectionately to Mary and Dorothy and give my little name sake and his sister [5] a kiss for me and believe me to be

Your Affection^{e} Broth[*line*]
JOHN WORDSWORTH

48. To Captain John Wordsworth

Address: John Wordsworth Esqr / Mascalls Hotel / Adelphi / London
Postmarks: PORTSMOUTH 73; G JAN 30 1805

Portsmouth Ship Abergavenny Jany 28th 1804 [*for* 1805]
My dear Cousin

I have received Sailing Instructions from his Majestys Frigate the Weymouth of 44 Guns and we had expected to sail this morning but as it blows a heavy Gale of Wind at SE it would be impossible to move the ship, I very much fear the wind is likely to draw round from the

Westward, when this gale has finishd, I wish most sincerely that we were off, as it will be of the greatest consequence to me to arrive in Bengal the first ship—

Mr Stewart has not yet given me Mr Wallace's notes to you but when we arrive in China you may depend upon my paying every attention to Mr W.'s commission in my power, and may assure him of the same— The Kings and Companys troops, 160 in all, are embarked and we are ⟨all⟩ ready for Sea whenever the Signal for sailing is made— the Soldiers Officers I have not yet seen, nor heard from, or of, any of them except one neither do I know the number I am to have

I forgot to tell Mr Dent when I wrote him yesterday, that the Ratcatcher is on board & I think he will destroy all the rats. We are but very indifferently manned our petty officers are ^all^ good men but the rest are only *trash*— tho bad as we are, I believe we are better ⟨manned⟩ off than any ship of the Season I could get men here and very good men but if I was *caught* shipping men that belonged to the Navy I should be dismissd the Service—[1] ⟨Joseph is very well⟩ The Ship makes two Inches water an hour which is near the same she made last voyage Mr Dents reason for being angry with me for not writing to him from in the Downs is certainly without cause for I knew no more of the extent of the damage of the Warren Hastings or the alarm she had created in town by sending a messenger than Mr Dent could know that we had received little or no damage, ^when he heard how the Warren Hastings had suffer'd—^ & I did not think it necessary to put the ship to the expence of sending a messenger or letter which might have ⟨amounted to⟩ ^cost^ as much ^money^ as the damage we had sustained. for the Gale lasted till within a few hours of our leaving the Downs. and you know at those times what advantages the Deal men would take of us.—

Joseph is very well, and I hope will continue so, as he was a good deal upon the Gun Deck about the Cables he did not feel so much of the cold and Wet as some of the other officers— I am much obliged to you for saying you will write to me by the China Direct Ships and at St Helena for I promise myself much pleasure from those Letters— I hope we shall be able to do something with Ponqua a[t] least I shall do every thing in my power and Mr Pottle who has a relation in the ship has promis'd me every assis{tance} he can give— I have also a letter to Larkins from M{r} Twining—and a very handsome one it is— he read {it to} me, at least, that part which concern'd myself, before he sealed it. Your time keeper went very well in the Down[s] as well as any timekeeper in the ship—

We are all hurry and confusion on board in consequence of the accident ⟨and it has the⟩ as the Carpenters have all been employ'd in making the necessary repairs about the bows instead of putting up Cabins shifting bulkheads &c—

Give my kindest remembrance and love to Mrs Wordsworth & I am dear Cousin

Yours Affectionately
JOHN WORDSWORTH

If we fall in with the Caroline Frigate I shall endeavour to see our cousin Charles Robinson [2] and deliver his Mothers letter myself.—

49. To Christopher Wordsworth

Address: Revd Christ^r Wordsworth / Oby near / Norwich [1] / Norfolk [2]

Postmarks: PORTSMOUTH 73; ⟨ ⟩ FEB ⟨ ⟩

Ship Abergany
[Portsmouth,] 31st Jany 1805

My dear Brother

We are at Portsmouth and expect to sail tomorrow Wind and Weather permitting I am sorry I could not have the pleasure of seeing you in Norfolk but my time would not permit me. I shall look forward with a great deal of pleasure to the time when we shall meet again and if I have the good fortune to arrive in England safe I will threaten you with the first visit— I have a family of 35 to provide for a[t] present which I ^you^ may ⟨imagain⟩ suppose must give me a great deal of trouble—

I have written this short letter principally to take ⟨bid⟩ Farewell to you and *my sister* [3] to whom I beg my kindest remembrances

I am My Dear Brother Your[s] Aff^ly
JOHN WORDSWORTH

50. To Captain John Wordsworth [1]

Address: Captn Wordsworth / Mascalls Hotel / Adelphi / London

Postmarks: PORTSMOUTH 73; ⟨ ⟩ FEB 3 1805

[Portsmouth,] 11 oclock p.m 31st Jany 1804 [*for* 1805]
My dear Cousin,

The Wind continues fair and we are to proceed to sea

tomorrow morning at daylight   the Commodore intends to go through the Needles a passage I do not like much but I hope will be attended with no accident, I am very much pleased with all my passengers and think we shall be as comfortab[l]e indeed far more so than I first expected, Captn Hipseley [2] (I do not know that I spell his name right) ⟨Com⟩ whom you perhaps remember at Bath, at least he knows you, commands the Troops   he seems to be a very moderate sensible man & I like him much—

Mr Evans & his family are ⟨as⟩ moderate in their wishes and expectations and *seem⟨ed⟩* to be pleased with *me* and the Ship   Mr Routledge [3] is as good and quiet a man as ever took a passage in an Indiaman—

Indeed I think we shall *do* far beyond my first expectation, I mean when we get clear of the Land and a little sett[l]ed, if we do not, I fear it will be my fault—

I am little used to company and shall feel myself *not a*[*t*] *home* ⟨for a⟩ at the first but I trust that will soon wear off—

Give my kindest Rememberances to Mrs Wordsworth

I am Dear Cousin

Yours very Affectionately
JOHN WORDSWORTH

⟨I shall⟩
I am sorry to say that we are obliged to leave this place without Mr Baggot and Mr Wordsworth

J. W

and it is not possible they can join the ship [4]

J. W

51. To Charles Thomas Coggan [1]

Address: Charles Thomas Coggan Esqr / East India House / London /
Below, in corner: Feby 1st / 5. PM [2]
Postmark: None

Ship Earl of Abergavenny
Motherbank Feby 1st 1805— [3]

Sir

I beg leave to Accquaint you that the Ship Earl of Abergavenny, is now under Weigh all well—in Company with His Majesty's Ship Weymouth—and to Enclose you a List of the Ships Company, & Passengers, with a list of the Water and Provisions on board [4]

I am
Sir Your Most Obed^{t} & Oblige[d]
JOHN WORDSWORTH

Chas Thos Coggan Esqr
E. I. House
London

NOTES

Abbreviations

AN — *An Authentic Narrative of the Loss of the Earl of Abergavenny, East Indiaman, Captain John Wordsworth* . . . By a Gentleman in the East-India House. London, 1805.

CC — Christopher Crackanthorpe (born Cookson), uncle of John Wordsworth.

CN — Burgoyne, G. A. *A Correct Narrative of the Loss of the Earl of Abergavenny East Indiaman, J. Wordsworth, Esq. Commander, Which Foundered in Weymouth Roads, on Tuesday Night, February the 5th, 1805.* Weymouth, n.d.

Coburn — Coburn, Kathleen (ed.). *The Notebooks of Samuel Taylor Coleridge.* 2 double vols. New York, 1957–61.

Cotton — Cotton, Evan. *East Indiamen: The East India Company's Maritime Service,* ed. Charles Fawcett. London, 1949.

CW — Christopher Wordsworth, brother of John Wordsworth.

DCP — Manuscripts in the Dove Cottage Library, Grasmere, microfilmed by Cornell University Library.

DW — Dorothy Wordsworth, sister of John Wordsworth.

DWJ — Darbishire, Helen (ed.). *Journals of Dorothy Wordsworth.* London, 1958.

EY — de Selincourt, Ernest (ed.). *The Letters of William and Dorothy Wordsworth: The Early Years 1787–1805.* Revised by Chester L. Shaver. Oxford, 1967. Figures refer to page numbers.

G — Letter from Thomas Gilpin to WW, April 25, 1805, in reply to one from WW, March 16 (DCP).

GGW — Manuscript biography of JW by Gordon Graham Wordsworth (DCP).

GM — "Loss of the *Abergavenny,*" *Gentleman's Magazine,* LXXV, Part 1 (February, 1805), 174–175.

Grosart — Grosart, A. B. (ed.). *The Prose Works of William Wordsworth.* 3 vols. London, 1876.

Gramshaw — Letter from "S. G." describing the adventures of Cadet Gramshaw in the wreck of the *Abergavenny. Gentleman's Magazine,* LXXV, Part 1 (March, 1805), 232.

Healey — *The Cornell Wordsworth Collection: A Catalogue of Books and Manuscripts Presented to the University by Mr. Victor Emanuel, Cornell 1919.* Compiled by George Harris Healey. Ithaca, New York, 1957.

IOR — India Office Records.

JW — John Wordsworth.

L — Lucas, E. V. (ed.). *The Letters of Charles Lamb, To Which Are Added Those of His Sister Mary Lamb.* 3 vols. New Haven, 1935. Figures refer to page numbers.

LY — de Selincourt, Ernest (ed.). *The Letters of William and Dorothy Wordsworth: The Later Years.* 3 vols. Oxford, 1939. Figures refer to page numbers.

Memoirs — Wordsworth, Christopher. *Memoirs of William Wordsworth, Poet-Laureate, D.C.L.* 2 vols. London, 1851.

Moorman — Moorman, Mary. *William Wordsworth, a Biography.* 2 vols. Oxford, 1965–1966.

Morse — Morse, Hosea B. *The Chronicles of the East India Company Trading to China, 1635–1834.* 5 vols. Oxford, 1926–1929.

MW — Burton, Mary E. (ed.). *The Letters of Mary Wordsworth.* Oxford, 1958. Figures refer to page numbers.

MY — de Selincourt, Ernest (ed.). *The Letters of William and Dorothy Wordsworth: The Middle Years.* 2 vols. Oxford, 1937. Figures refer to page numbers.

NL — *An Authentic Narrative of the Loss of the Earl of Abergavenny, East Indiaman, off Portland . . . Corrected from the Official Returns at the East-India House.* London, 1805. Cover title: *Narrative of the Loss of the Earl of Abergavenny East-Indiaman.*

Parkinson — Parkinson, C. Northcote. *Trade in the Eastern Seas, 1793–1813.* Cambridge, 1937.

Prelude — Wordsworth, William. *The Prelude; or, Growth of a Poet's Mind,* ed. Ernest de Selincourt and Helen Darbishire. Oxford, 1959. Line references are to 1850 version, unless otherwise noted.

PW — de Selincourt, Ernest, and Helen Darbishire (eds.) *The Poetical Works of William Wordsworth.* 5 vols. Oxford, 1940–1949. Figures refer to page numbers.

Reed — Reed, Mark L. *Wordsworth: The Chronology of the Early Years, 1770–1799.* Cambridge, Mass., 1967.

RW	Richard Wordsworth, brother of John Wordsworth.
SH	Coburn, Kathleen (ed.). *The Letters of Sara Hutchinson, from 1800 to 1835.* Toronto, 1954. Figures refer to page numbers.
STC	Griggs, Earl Leslie (ed.). *Collected Letters of Samuel Taylor Coleridge.* 4 vols. Oxford, 1956–1959. Figures refer to page numbers.
WP	Wordsworth family papers used by permission of a person who wishes to remain anonymous.
WW	William Wordsworth.
Y	Letter from Midshipman Benjamin Yates, March 31, 1805, to cousin in the India House, in reply to questions transmitted by Charles Lamb. Lamb sent the letter on to Wordsworth with his own comment added.

Introduction

1. DCP. The actual date of the wreck was the 5th.

2. *EY* 540, 543, 552, 553, 558, 591, 594, 598–599, 649, 659.

3. *MY* 189.

4. *EY* 577. "The news . . . has disordered me from head to foot," Southey wrote to C. W. W. Wynn on February 13 (*Life and Correspondence of Robert Southey,* ed. Charles Southey [London, 1850], II, 321). To Wordsworth he wrote: "It has been my custom when in affliction to force myself to mental exertion, a difficult thing—but possible.—but it made my sleep dreadful.—for grief—as far as it is a bodily feeling the disease will have its course" (DCP).

5. *L* I, 382. Mary Lamb sent Dorothy "some poor lines . . . written . . . with strong feeling" under the conviction "that you would see every object with, and through your lost brother, and that that would at last become a real and everlasting source of comfort to you. . . .":

> Why is he wandering on the sea?
> Coleridge should now with Wordsworth be.
>
> . . . . .
>
> He'd tell them that their brother dead
> When years have passed o'er their head,
> Will be remember'd with such holy,
> True, and perfect melancholy

That ever this lost brother John
Will be their heart's companion.

(*L* I, 392–393.)

6. *STC* 1165, 1170; *Coburn* II, Text, Item 2517. "Never yet has any Loss gone so far into the Life of Hope, with me," Coleridge wrote six days after hearing the news (Item 2527).

7. A final letter from JW, dated February 1 (Letter 51) survives in the India Office, and he wrote one after that date which has not survived.

8. DCP (Wordsworth family Bible).

9. Eric Robertson, *Wordsworthshire: An Introduction to a Poet's Country* (London, 1911), p. 26, mistakenly states that the Cockermouth Church register does not mention John's baptism. It is recorded, however, both at Cockermouth Church (*Reed* 41) and in a copy of the register which I have examined in the Cumberland County Archives at Carlisle.

10. DCP.

11. *L* I, 315.

12. *Prelude* I, line 290.

13. *EY* 564.

14. *Memoirs* I, 33.

15. DCP (rent book of John Wordsworth, Sr.).

16. Their father paid board for three boys to Hugh Tyson on June 16, 1782 (DCP, rent book).

17. *Ibid.*

18. Ann Tyson's ledger is preserved in Hawkshead Grammar School. The entries cited are on pp. 31, 37, 40, and 42.

19. MS version of *Poems on the Naming of Places,* VI (DCP).

20. "The Brothers," lines 47–49, 61–64 (*PW* II, 2).

21. *Prelude* III, lines 359, 369–370.

22. *MY* 118.

23. *EY* 562–563.

24. XII, lines 287 ff.

25. *Reed* 59, citing Cockermouth Parish Records.

26. WP.

27. *EY* 3–5.

28. *EY* 3.

29. WP (CC's accounts).

30. *EY* 11.

31. WP (Accounts of Richard Wordsworth of Whitehaven, JW's uncle).

32. *EY* 16.

33. WP; *EY* 23.

34. WP; *EY* 23.

35. In a letter to CC which he subsequently dated July, 1790, RW wrote, ". . . The Carlisle is at Dover the Ship in which my Brother John sailed. . . . I shall make enquiry after him and find him out as soon as he arrives in the River" (WP). The date, which RW added when reviewing his correspondence with his uncle some years later, is inaccurate, for JW was on his way to China in July, 1790. Probably the correct year was 1789. I can find no record of the arrival of a ship named the *Carlisle* for that year, but on July 6 a ship of that name was in the Downs bound for America under Captain Corner. Since a Captain Corner is mentioned in a pamphlet on the wreck of the *Abergavenny* as the East India Company's Master Attendant, and since JW in Letter 26 implies that he has a firsthand knowledge of America, it is likely that Richard was mistaken about the month also and that JW sailed with the *Carlisle* on her July voyage or the one just preceding.

36. WP (CC to RW).

37. WP (Richard Wordsworth of Branthwaite, JW's cousin, to RW in London, October 31, 1789).

38. WP (CC to RW, December 18, 1789).

39. *Recollections of the Table-Talk of Samuel Rogers* (New York, 1856), 258 n.; *Moorman* I, 124–125; *Reed* 95.

40. Arthur Machen, "Introduction," *The Expedition of Humphry Clinker,* by Tobias Smollett (New York, 1929), ix;

Survey Gazetteer of the British Isles, ed. John Bartholomew (Edinburgh, 1952), s.v. "Abergavenny."

41. The *Abergavenny*'s outward-bound invoice from London in 1790 included (besides items intended for the ship's use) sword blades, boots, books, beaver skins, "burning canes," corks, confectionery, cutlery, cochineal, camlets, coney skins, fox hounds, water engines, silver cream ewers, enamel boxes, mahogany furniture, feathers, ship's figureheads, window glass, gloves, guns, glass beads, hats, haberdashery, hose, herbs, iron and steel bars, knee buckles, knives, looking-glasses, lead, lace, music, musical instruments, otter skins, perfumery and powder, prints, painter's colors, rattans, tennis rackets and balls, silk hose, stationery, shoe buckles, shot, toys, tin, tea, whale line cordage, Wedgwood ware, and whips (WP). Much of this, of course, was for the Company's employees in India.

42. IOR (Log 341A).

43. IOR (Ledger and receipt book 341G).

44. WP (RW to CC, April 21, 1790).

45. *EY* 60.

46. WP.

47. *EY* 66.

48. WP (CC to RW, March 8, 1792).

49. *EY* 73.

50. *EY* 78 & n.

51. *EY* 79.

52. WP.

53. WP (Rev. Thomas Myers to RW, May 23, 1792; CC to RW, June 14).

54. DCP (to Richard Wordsworth of Whitehaven, John Wordsworth's uncle).

55. *STC* 732.

56. He may have returned by late February, 1793, if, as Reed suggests, the tailor's bill then paid for him by his uncle represented a recent purchase (WP; *Reed* 133 & n.).

57. *Cotton* 33 & n. The tonnage figures are for the years following 1796.

58. WP (Captain Wordsworth's trade book); Michael Greenberg, *British Trade and the Opening of China 1800–1842* (Cambridge, 1951), p. 5.

59. WP (Captain Wordsworth's trade book; homeward manifest of the *Abergavenny* from China).

60. IOR (Log 341B).

61. DCP (to WW).

62. *EY* 136.

63. GGW.

64. IOR (Ledger and receipt book 341H).

65. *Moorman* I, 260 ff.; *Reed* 162 ff.

66. GGW.

67. IOR (Log 400N).

68. IOR (Marine Miscellaneous Series, Vol. 657, p. 214).

69. IOR (Ledger and receipt book 400AA).

70. The loan was received on April 28 (DCP, accounts between RW and William Crackanthorpe).

71. DCP (RW to WW, May 3, 1797).

72. DCP (RW to WW).

73. IOR (Log 775E).

74. *EY* 270.

75. IOR (Ledger and receipt book 775L).

76. GGW.

77. *Ibid.*

78. *Reed* 273; *EY* 271.

79. *EY* 271.

80. *Prelude* IV, 22.

81. *EY* 272.

82. *Coburn* I, Text, Item 514.

83. *EY* 272.

84. *EY* 4.

85. *EY* 563.

86. *Coburn* I, Text, Items 555, 798.

87. *STC* 543.

88. *EY* 649.

89. *Ibid.*

90. *EY* 559–560.

91. *EY* 559.

92. DCP (MS version of *Poems on the Naming of Places,* VI, lines 63–66).

93. *DWJ,* March 4, 1802.

94. *MW* 3.

95. *EY* 560.

96. *EY* 571, 560.

97. See WW's later descriptive poems, "Malham Cove" (*PW* III, 37); "Gordale" (*ibid.*)

98. *EY* 295–296, 361, 622.

99. *EY* 556.

100. *EY* 2.

101. "Elegiac Verses in Memory of My Brother, John Wordsworth," lines 22–24 (*PW* IV, 264).

102. *EY* 598. The story told by John Wilson ("Christopher North") that, as the brothers' "last act" at Grisedale Tarn, "they agreed to lay the foundation-stone of a little fishing-hut, and this they did with tears" is apparently a fantasy based on "Michael." See Robertson, *Wordsworthshire,* p. 325.

103. *DWJ* (September 29, 1800).

104. C. H. Philips, *The East India Company, 1784–1834* (Manchester, 1961), p. 86 & n.

105. GGW.

106. IOR (Marine Miscellaneous Series, Vol. 657, p. 214).

107. IOR (Court Minutes).

108. *Ibid.*

109. *Cotton* 28.

110. DCP.

111. WP (Robert Griffith to William Threlkeld of Halifax, Yorkshire).

112. *Morse* II, 72.

113. *Morse* II, 347.

114. GGW, based on RW's accounts. WW (*EY* 563) said the amount was "about £1,000."

115. IOR (Log 341E).

116. Robert Southey, when he met Wordsworth's French daughter in 1817, observed that "she is a very interesting young woman, with much more of natural feeling than of French manners, and surprizingly like John Wordsworth, much more so than his own sister." *New Letters of Robert Southey,* ed. Kenneth Curry (New York and London, 1965), II, 161 (to Mrs. Southey, May 17). He later repeated the remark to DW (*MY* 801).

117. *EY* 375–376.

118. WP (RW to correspondent unknown).

119. DCP (February 12, 1803).

120. DCP. RW deducted £100 for law expenses. He also urged WW to try to borrow one or two thousand pounds from his friends on JW's behalf, adding, "I have been much cramped, by what I advanced, & I wish in future not to be so confined in this particular as I was during John's last voyage" (DCP, February 14, 1803). WW did try to borrow £1500, but failed (*EY* 385).

121. *EY* 387.

122. DCP.

123. *EY* 388.

124. DCP; RW to James Graham, February 12, 1803 (DCP), and to Lord Lowther, March 30, 1803 (WP), re payment of £3000 for JW's use; *EY* 546. RW's accounts with WW and DW evidently do not record in detail the true state of affairs. Sara Hutchinson, on June 29, 1815, wrote that "W[m]'s money we suspect—indeed R[d] Addison said as much—is already invested in R[d] W's Land. But no answer is to be had from him" (*SH* 81, to Mrs. Hutchinson of Hindwell). Among other investments, Richard had bought 1/50 of Penrith Race Course in 1811 (WP).

125. E. K. Chambers, *Samuel Taylor Coleridge: A Biographical Study* (Oxford, 1938), pp. 163–166, speculates on this possibility, suggesting that Coleridge in 1803 may have believed that Sara's nervousness was connected with the pros-

pect of her marriage to JW. *SH* xxvi states that "family tradition has it, supported by an entry in one of Coleridge's notebooks, that John Wordsworth wished, or the family wished him, to marry Sara." But George Whalley, *Coleridge and Sara Hutchinson and the Asra Poems* (London, 1955), p. 54 n., says that "the tradition in the Wordsworth family, even at the present time, is that John was in love with *Mary,* and that his unpublished letters show that he was bitterly disappointed by the news of William's betrothal to her." The two reported traditions are not, of course, incompatible, but the former seems traceable entirely to Coleridge.

126. *EY* 563.

127. *MY* 425.

128. *Coburn* II, Notes, Item 2975. Coleridge later admitted in a memorandum that the episode had been pure fantasy: "I *knew* the horrid phantasm to be a mere phantasm: and yet what anguish, what gnawings of despair, what throbbings and lancinations of positive Jealousy!—even to this day the undying worm of distempered Sleep or morbid Day-dreams" (*ibid.*)

129. *Coburn* II, Text, Item 2861.

130. *Coburn* II, Text, Item 2517.

131. Loaned in 1801 (GGW).

132. WP (bond to Reverend Thomas Bowley, Queens College, Oxford). Interest on the bond was paid through 1807.

133. WP.

134. *Morse* II, "East India Company's Ships at Canton, 1775–1804."

135. "Interesting Intelligence from the London Gazettes," *Gentleman's Magazine,* LXXIV, Part 2 (1804), 963.

136. "Abstract of Foreign Occurrences: France," *Gentleman's Magazine,* LXXIV, Part 2 (1804), 967.

137. *Ibid.*

138. IOR (Court Minutes, August 15, 1804, Vol. 113, pp. 647–648; Miscellanies, August 22, 1804, Vol. 44).

139. IOR (Ledger 341L).

140. IOR (Log 341F).

141. DCP.

142. *Cotton* 73.

143. As might be expected, accounts of the *Abergavenny*'s last voyage differ from each other in many details, including the matter of the formal leave-taking. The pamphlet which I refer to as *NL* attributes JW's delay to "an unaccountable depression of spirits," which caused him to avoid the ceremony until the Wednesday following the day originally set for it, when he "yielded to the wishes of his friends, and reluctantly attended the Court!" (p. 49). The pamphlet *AN* denies this, explaining that "those who are in the habit of attending the India House, know that the forms of office are ever strictly adhered to; those forms were not completed, and Captain WORDSWORTH was obliged to defer his parting obeisance till another day" (p. 29). Finally, for what the information is worth, John Barlow of Weymouth, author of a blank-verse poem *The Loss of the Earl of Abergavenny, East-Indiaman* (Weymouth, n.d.), claimed to have been "most credibly informed that Captain Wordsworth, previous to his departure, was so elated with the hopes of a prosperous voyage, that his friends expressed a concern at his unusual flow of spirits" (p. 6 n.).

Such contradictions make it necessary to assess the evidence concerning the wreck rather carefully. It may be appropriate at this point to give a brief list of the sources available. A number of these have been reviewed by Professor E. L. McAdam, Jr., in his article "Wordsworth's Shipwreck," *PMLA,* LXXVII (1962), 240–247, an excellent account of the ways in which several of the published descriptions of the wreck shed light on WW's anxiety about his brother's conduct. Professor McAdam's quotations indicate that the pamphlets to which he refers correspond to two of three pamphlets in the Dove Cottage Library. The earliest of the three, *An Authentic Narrative of the Loss of the Earl of Abergavenny* (*NL* in my notes), dated February 13 by Professor McAdam, was published by John Stockdale and Blacks and Parry. The Dove Cottage copy belonged to Thomas Cookson, Sara Hutchinson's friend at Kendal, whose signature appears on the cover. Apparently Sara, DW, or WW had asked Mr. Cookson to find them a copy of the *second* pamphlet, perhaps identifying it by its motto (as DW did in a letter to Mrs. Marshall, March 15 and 17, 1805, *EY* 560–561): Sara wrote Mr. Cookson to thank him for "the Narrative" of the wreck, but said it "was certainly the wrong one" (Jonathan Wordsworth, "Letters of the Coleridge Circle," *Times Literary Supplement,* February 15, 1968). Sara added that "we had already seen many copies of the other"—that is, the one they had originally asked for, a Minerva Press pamphlet, almost identical in title with the first, which Professor McAdam dates February 21 (*AN* in my notes). The Dove Cottage copy of this pamphlet lacks the title page, with its cruel motto from Clarence's dream in *Richard III,* and the preface by William Dalmeida of the East India Company (*EY* 560–561 n.). *AN* attacks the "gross inaccuracies" of *NL* and contradicts certain of its points, though many passages in the two are identical. Several factual corrections have been written into *AN* by WW. A third pamphlet in the Dove Cottage collection, not cited by Professor McAdam, *Correct Statement of the Loss of the Earl of Abergavenny . . . also the Shipwreck of Occum Chamnan: a Siamese Noble,* derives chiefly from *NL* or its sources and has no independent value. There are also various newspaper accounts.

For my own description of the wreck I have drawn whenever possible on narratives by eyewitnesses. Three of these are by Fourth Mate Thomas Gilpin: his official report to the India House (*AN* 10–12 and *L* I, 388–389); his letter to Charles Lamb (*L* I, 391), and his letter to WW (G). The India House report is a detailed, self-consistent narrative by an experienced seaman and can generally be relied upon. It is supplemented, however, and at one key point contradicted, by a pamphlet (*CN*) issued by Cornet G. A. Burgoyne, who also had been at sea for several years. Midshipman Benjamin Yates, in a letter to a cousin in the India House (Y), answered several questions about the wreck, put to him, through the cousin, by Charles Lamb. A passenger, Thomas Evans, wrote to WW giving a general description of JW's conduct on the voyage (*EY* 581–582). Midshipman William White left a brief narrative of the sinking (*AN* 53–54). Finally, there is a vivid account in the *Gentleman's Magazine* of the experiences of one of the cadets on the night of the wreck (*Gramshaw*).

144. *NL* 7; *CN* 4.

145. *AN* 7; *CN* 5. Two of the three occupants of the sloop, First Mate Samuel Baggot and Ensign Whitlow, were drowned when the *Abergavenny* sank; the third, JW's cousin Joseph Wordsworth, was saved.

146. Fourth Mate Thomas Gilpin's memorandum to the Court of Directors, *AN* 10. Except where otherwise noted, I have followed this account.

147. DCP (on a copy of *The St. James's Chronicle, or British Evening-Post,* February 7 to 9, 1805, containing an account of the wreck).

148. IOR (Court Minutes, February 6, 1805, Vol. 113A, p. 1396).

149. *CN* 6.

150. G.

151. G.

152. *EY* 564.

153. *AN* 9.

154. G.

155. For an expert opinion on this point I have consulted Mr. Reginald Riggs, Station Officer, Her Majesty's Coastguard, Portland Bill, Dorset. I am indebted to Mr. Riggs for local information about the waters off Portland, and for calling my attention to *CN*. Mr. Riggs agrees that the lull in the

wind was responsible for the wreck; he adds, however, that the disaster might have been averted if the pilot had steered farther south before heading eastward. The question, then, becomes one of judgment as to how much preparation the pilot ought to have made for the emergency that actually arose. If his marks were open, he was on a standard course.

156. Reports that JW had at first neglected to fire signal guns (e.g., *AN* 12) were among several details in the accounts of the wreck that distressed WW, who desperately needed reassurance that his brother's conduct had been equal to the occasion. Gilpin's memorandum, however, clearly stated that guns were fired "from the time she struck till she went down." See *EY* 557.

157. *NL* 48.

158. *NL* 48 gives the height of the water at this point as 6–8 feet.

159. Y. The failure to launch the boats sooner was a second point in the accounts of the wreck (e.g., *NL* 11) which troubled WW. In addition to Yates's explanations, Gilpin's report states that the longboat could not have been reached without laying the main-topsail aback and delaying progress (*AN* 11). Burgoyne, however, denies this, saying that the after sails had been lowered (*CN* 7–8). Yates's statement that the jib and the foresail were kept up seems to confirm Burgoyne, but JW's final order to "haul on board the main tack" may mean that the mainsail was not lowered, only loose. Burgoyne adds that there was a cutter hanging to the starboard quarter that was never launched; at the end she was filled with men, but she went down with the ship (*CN* 8–9). *AN* 24 reports that Seaman Webber was saved by swimming to a ship's launch containing sheep and a cow.

On the whole, the evidence suggests at least a strong possibility that, even if Gilpin's reason is mistaken, JW's apparent neglect of the boats was the result of a deliberate decision, based, as Yates suggests, on two considerations: the need of enough manpower to keep the *Abergavenny* afloat and moving toward shore, and the danger from the swell, "the short lop of the sea" which prevented the sloop's boat from returning after rescuing the first load of passengers, and persuaded at least one of the passengers that she was safer aboard the ship (*CN* 7).

160. *AN* 13. *CN* 6 attributes the rise of the water to the breaking of the large pumps.

161. Y.

162. Y.

163. *CN* 7; *NL* 10.

164. *CN* 7; *AN* 14.

165. *EY* 582 (Thomas Evans to WW, quoted by DW to Lady Beaumont).

166. Y; G.

167. *AN* 16.

168. Jonathan Wordsworth, "A Wordsworth Letter," *Times Literary Supplement,* July 27, 1967, p. 673 (WW to Robert Southey, late March-early April, 1805, after conversation with Captain Wordsworth, Sr., who had talked with the Evanses in London; see *EY* 582. From a copy by Mrs. Christopher Wordsworth made in preparation for the *Memoirs.*)

169. *NL* 9.

170. *GM.*

171. *NL* 11.

172. *AN* 17; *NL* 17. *NL* gives his words as "Let her go! God's will be done" and says that he uttered them "with every appearance of a heart-broken man." *AN,* however, says that "The Captain and Mr. BAGGOT were observed to converse with apparent cheerfulness"—a detail that Lamb transmitted to WW (*L* I, 388, March 5, 1805) and which DW quoted with evident satisfaction to Jane Marshall (*EY* 559).

173. G. It was variously reported that Baggot was drowned in a vain attempt to save a passenger, Mrs. Blair (*NL* 14–15)

or overpowered by the sea as he tried to reach the longboat stowed in the booms (*CN* 13).

174. *L* I, 430–431 (Mary Lamb to Catherine Clarkson, March 13, 1806). Mrs. Clarkson had heard reports of JW's drunkenness, apparently from an underwriter. Mary Lamb denies the reports categorically, saying that no blame was attached to JW by the Directors or elsewhere in the India House, and that the underwriters always blame the captain for the loss of a ship. She traces the rumor to the story of the two glasses of liquor, "told at the India House" by Burgoyne. Apparently Charles Lamb did not interview Burgoyne at the time Burgoyne gave this account; Charles and Mary tried to find him afterward, but failed. However, Burgoyne wrote his own description of the wreck, which was published at Weymouth (*CN*). His only mention of the episode is as follows: "Having some hollands on board, I served each man pumping and bailing, with a dram to cheer their drooping spirits." Burgoyne was in Weymouth on two different occasions, having returned after the wreck to claim some property (*AN* 27).

175. *AN* 26; G.

176. *NL* 11–12; *AN* 12, 53; *Gramshaw.*

177. Y.

178. *AN* 24. Yates, however, who claimed to have seen the Captain the instant the ship went down, made no mention of the hencoop, and Gilpin contradicted Webber's story that JW was washed overboard.

179. *Gramshaw.*

180. G.

181. *GM* puts the figure at 80 or 90, *AN* 18 at 180.

182. *AN* 53–54.

183. Gilpin to Charles Lamb, March 31, 1805, in *L* I, 391 (Lamb to WW, April 5, 1805); G. As Professor McAdam points out, WW was appalled by the newspaper accounts which said that JW did not seem to wish to outlive the disaster. Lamb lied at least once to spare WW's feelings: he told him that *AN* "confirms Gilpin's account of his seeing

your brother striving to save himself" (*L* I, 388), whereas *AN* repeats the *Times*'s statement that "Mr. Gilpin . . . used every persuasion to induce him to endeavour to save his life . . . he did not seem desirous to survive the loss of his ship" (McAdam, *op. cit.,* pp. 241–243). Lamb was careful not to send the pamphlet to WW. He did send him Yates's letter (Y) in which Yates expressed his opinion that JW "never had a wish to survive the loss of his property," but Lamb added a note deprecating the remark: "Your own knowledge of your Brother will tell you to { } can belong to this young seaman's surmises. . . . {He} did not know, as you did the inner man." Lamb also reported that Gilpin, in an interview, had assured him "that your Brother did try to save himself, and was doing so when Gilpin called to him, but he was then struggling with the waves and almost dead" (*L* I, 384). Gilpin's other statements, it may be noted, mention no struggle beyond the brief effort to cling to a rope. WW, however, took great comfort from Lamb's reassurance and from Gilpin's statement in his letter to Lamb that JW had survived the sinking by as much as five minutes (*EY* 583). In several letters WW refers to JW's attempts to save himself (*EY* 547, 564, 583); and under the passage in *AN* 24 stating that JW did not wish to survive his ship, WW has written, "Contradicted by Gilpin, who spoke to Capt Wordsworth—and saw him using every exertion to save his Life.—"

184. *Gramshaw.*

185. *CN* 15–23 (survivor lists). *NL* 13 states that many persons were washed from the rigging or lost their grip in the cold. Burgoyne (*CN* 14) denies this, and the figures in *GM*, plus the statement in *NL* 13 that the sloop's boat "returned three times, taking twenty each turn," seem to bear him out. *AN* 20 gives the hour when the rescue began at about midnight; Gilpin's official report says 2 A.M.

186. *NL* 15–16.

187. IOR (Ledger and Receipt Book 341L, containing petition with endorsement; Court Minutes, Vol. 113A,

pp. 1415, 1446–1447, 1749 ff., Vol. 114, pp. 17–18; Minutes of the Committee of Correspondence, Vol. 2, February 26, 1805).

188. IOR (Court Minutes, Vol. 113A, pp. 1457–1458, 1467, 1487, 1754–1755; Vol. 114, p. 479; Vol. 115, pp. 147–148; Vol. 115A, p. 808). An account of the diving apparatus used to recover property from the wreck is given in the *Monthly Magazine,* XXI (1806). Edward Ferguson's report that the *Abergavenny* had been raised in July, 1805 (*EY* 619 n.) was apparently mistaken.

189. This and the preceding passage (p. 49) are from "To the Daisy," lines 46–52 (*PW* IV, 262).

190. C. H. Stewart to Captain John Wordsworth, Sr., March 22, 1805; *Gentleman's Magazine,* LXXV, Part 1 (1805), 295. Stewart was acting as agent for the underwriters of the *Abergavenny*. He concludes his letter by informing Captain Wordsworth that he has offered a reward for JW's sword. It was recovered and now belongs to WW's great-great-grandson Richard Wordsworth (*EY* 571 n.). Sara Hutchinson states that it was "an aunt of Mr. C. Wordsworth" who gave directions for the funeral (*SH* 7, to Mrs. Cookson, March 26, 1805).

191. DCP (Gordon Graham Wordsworth to Mrs. C. King-Warry, June 16, 1932, citing an interview with the rector at Wyke Regis).

192. "It is a well known fact that whenever a Ship is lost the underwriters always blame the Captains" (Mary Lamb to Catherine Clarkson, citing Charles Lamb, *L* I, 431). On March 8, 1805, RW wrote to DW, "I have no reason to think that any of us shall suffer in our Property. . . . The Insurance was considible" (*EY* 552 n.). RW's accounts with WW and DW show no loss, but Gordon Graham Wordsworth's examination of RW's accounts on JW's behalf indicates that JW's creditors had to settle for 18*s*. in the pound (GGW).

193. IOR (Court Minutes, Vol. 113A, pp. 1426, 1508–1509).

194. IOR (Court Minutes, Vol. 115A, p. 1331).

195. *EY* 548; *Sara Coleridge and Henry Reed,* ed. Leslie N. Broughton (Ithaca, N.Y., 1937), pp. 74–75, 105. Sara also states that JW "was thought heavy & commonplace by general observers" (p. 104), and, after describing WW's eldest son John as dull, slow, and sluggish, goes on to say (with due precaution against scandal), "He seems to inherit the temperament of his Uncle Capt John Wordsworth (not *from* him of course). . . ." (p. 74). Sara's information is, we recall, second-hand (she was two when JW drowned); her remarks emphasize the fact that one needed to know JW well to know him at all. She is in effect stating the obverse of DW's remark to Lady Beaumont: "[John's] habits from childhood were shy and lonely in the extreme, so that if he had not had so much dignity of character he would to most have appeared odd" (*EY* 582).

196. *EY* 559 (DW to Jane Marshall, March 15 and 17, 1805).

197. *EY* 581–582 (in DW to Lady Beaumont, April 15, 1805). *NL* 16 states that JW "was considered one of the first navigators in the service."

198. *EY* 556.

199. *EY* 562.

200. WW said that JW was "respected and liked by every body that knew him" (*EY* 564, to James Losh, March 16, 1805). "He was a humane good Man & his Loss I shall regret," wrote Gilpin (G). "If he had returned, and settled in Life," wrote Thomas Clarkson, "he would have been useful in his Day, by the practical Duty of Benevolence, and by his Example to others." He went on to record that Wilberforce had grieved for JW for days (DCP, to WW, March 1, 1805). "John was the delight of all the Passengers," Captain Wordsworth, Sr. wrote to WW, after speaking to Mr. Evans (DCP, March 18, 1805).

201. *EY* 559.

202. *MY* 152.

203. As a young man WW, who had "always fancied that he had talents for command," had thought (apparently seriously) of taking up a military life, but was deterred by two practical considerations—lack of influence and the fear of yellow fever (reminiscences of Lady Richardson, November 8, 1845, *Grosart* III, 451–452). For an investigation of the theme of stoicism in WW's elegies on John's death, see R. C. Townsend, "John Wordsworth and his Brother's Poetic Development," *PMLA,* LXXXI (1966), 70–78.

204. *EY* 563.

205. "Resolution and Independence," lines 40–42 (*PW* II, 236).

206. See Z. S. Fink, ed., *The Early Wordsworthian Milieu* (Oxford, 1958).

207. *EY* 559; *PW* II, 122 (*Poems on the Naming of Places,* VI, line 80).

208. "His taste in all the arts, music and poetry in particular (for these he of course had had the best opportunities of being familiar with) was exquisite" (*EY* 548, WW to Sir George Beaumont). In an unfinished draft of an answer to a letter from Mr. Evans, passenger on the *Abergavenny,* WW wrote: "My Brother . . . was very fond of reading & had a most exquisite taste, in poetry in particular; & I well know the delight which he would have found in reading to the Young Ladies under your care, such passages as he admired" (DCP).

209. *MY* 7.

210. *EY* 313–314 (to Charles James Fox).

211. *Grosart* III, 165 (Fenwick note to "Character of the Happy Warrior").

212. WW told Mary and DW that, as Mary recorded, "it is only our pleasures and our joys that are broken in upon—but [this] loss of John is deeply connected with his *business*"

—that is, presumably, the business of poetry (*MW* 2, to Catherine Clarkson, March 7, 1805).

213. *EY* 556.

214. This reading, of course, emphasizes what seems to me the total impression conveyed by the imagery of the poem, rather than Wordsworth's formal repudiation of his earlier happiness as selfish and illusory.

The Letters

1–1. *A. Parkins Esq*ʳ: At this time RW was associated with Messrs. Parkin and Lambert.

1–2. The correct date of this letter, written from the home of JW's uncle Christopher Crackanthorpe (born Cookson; see Letter 2, Note 1), is established by the postmark and by a letter of July 31 from CC to RW, saying that JW had left the week before (WP).

1–3. Captain John Wordsworth was JW's first cousin, the son of Richard Wordsworth of Whitehaven, JW's father's brother. Some eighteen years older than JW, he had been a captain with the East India Company since 1782. He commanded the *Earl of Abergavenny* from 1789 until JW succeeded him in 1801.

1–4. *last voyage:* JW's first voyage on the *Earl of Abergavenny,* January, 1790–August, 1791.

1–5. *Kitt:* JW's younger brother Christopher, who had been visiting the Cooksons since the beginning of his holiday from Hawkshead School about June 17 (WP, CC to RW, June 14 and July 31, 1792).

1–6. *M*ʳ *Smith att Broughton:* The husband of Captain John Wordsworth's sister.

1–7. *M*ʳ *Barkers:* Francis Barker of Rampside was married to Elizabeth, the sister of Mrs. Smith of Broughton and of Captain John Wordsworth.

2–1. *Christopher Crackanthorpe:* After inheriting Newbiggin Hall near Penrith from his mother in 1792, JW's uncle dropped his father's name of Cookson, in honor of his mother's family, the Crackanthorpes, through whom the estate came to him. His full name became Christopher Crackanthorpe Crackanthorpe.

2–2. *on board of Ship:* In preparation for his second voyage with the *Earl of Abergavenny,* as fifth mate.

2–3. *That hundred pound of my sisters,* etc.: DW had offered JW this money, a gift from her maternal grandmother Dorothy Crackanthorpe Cookson, who had given JW £100 also. DW had transferred the sum to a Carlisle bank, wishing, she said, "to have the Interest within my Reach" (*EY* 80). The principal was still under the control of CC, though he asked for DW's written consent before having his agent send a draft for the amount to RW on May 16, 1793 (WP, CC to RW, March 8, 1792; CC to RW, April 30, 1793; RW to CC, May 1793).

2–4. *my wages in the ship,* etc.: JW's pay on this voyage was 45*s.* per month; his total wages after deductions came to £41 11*s.* 8*d.* for a voyage of 21 months (IOR, Ledger 341H).

2–5. "Protections" against impressment seem to have been regularly applied for by the Company, though this letter makes clear that they sometimes had little practical value. Thus on February 4, 1801, the Company applied to the Lords Commissioners of the Admiralty both for a protection for the *Earl of Abergavenny* and for "travelling protections" for her crewmen between the time they were recruited and the time they boarded the ship in the Thames (IOR, Miscellanies, Vol. 41).

2–6. *Miss Cust:* CC's sister-in-law. In 1787 Dorothy had called the Cust sisters "a mixture of Ignorance, Pride, affectation, self-conceit, and affected notability" (*EY* 10).

3–1. *Gallow Hill:* The farm rented by Mary Hutchinson's brother Thomas.

3–2. The last part of the word is scrawled illegibly down the edge of the sheet.

3–3. *Aunt Monkhouse:* Miss Elizabeth Monkhouse (1750–1828), the sister of Mary Hutchinson's mother. After the death of their parents, Mary and three of the younger Hutchinson children lived with Miss Monkhouse and a great-aunt until 1788 (*MW* xxi).

3–4. *Joanna:* Joanna Hutchinson (1780–1843), Mary Hutchinson's youngest sister, the subject of one of WW's *Poems on the Naming of Places.*

3–5. *Newbiggin:* See Letter 2, note 1.

3–6. *Mr Parkin,* etc.: In the negotiations for building a new ship "on the bottom" of the *Earl of Abergavenny* after it was wrecked in 1805, Hugh Parkin appears as the owner of a 1/16 share (*Parkinson* 187).

3–7. *Sara:* Sara Hutchinson, Mary's sister. For the relationships among Sara, Coleridge, and JW, see Introduction, pp. 35–36.

3–8. *I find the mail,* etc.: That is, after beginning his letter JW discovered that the mail coach in which he was travelling on his way from Penrith to London did not go as far east as York. Contemporary maps show a postal route from Penrith to York via Greta Bridge, and JW probably thought at first that this was the one he was to follow. See George Whalley, *Coleridge and Sara Hutchinson and the Asra Poems* (London, 1955), p. 37 n.

4–1. *Single:* This notified the postal clerk who marked the charges on the letter that it consisted of only a single sheet. Each sheet was charged at the same rate as a separate letter.

4–2. *Forncett:* JW's maternal uncle William Cookson was rector of Forncett and later canon of Windsor. DW had lived with her uncle and aunt and their increasing family at Forncett from December, 1788 until Christmas, 1793. The letter mentions five children by name; there were actually six—Mary, born 1790; Christopher, born 1791; William, born

1792; George, born 1793; Anna, born 1796; and Elizabeth, born 1797.

4–3. *when I was last at forncett:* He had been there from about December 30, 1791, to April 30, 1792.

4–4. *not very handsome:* Mary's earlier beauty had been striking enough to impress King George at Windsor in 1792, probably the same year JW had last seen her. "The King," wrote DW, "stopped to talk with my Uncle and Aunt, and to play with the children. . . . Mary he considers as a great beauty and desired the Duke of York to come from one Side of the Terrace to the other to look at her" (*EY* 83).

4–5. *the Crackanthorp family:* Canon Cookson's mother (JW's maternal grandmother) was born Dorothy Crackanthorpe.

4–6. *that Mr Wedgewood may be paid immediately:* On July 13, 1800, WW wrote to Josiah Wedgwood explaining that the debt of some £100 accumulated by WW in the course of his trip to Germany could now be repaid to Wedgwood without WW's selling his £270 in stocks. This was possible because Charles Douglass, a friend of Montagu, had recently paid half of the £200 lent him by WW in 1796 (*Moorman* I, 269; *EY* 183, 283, 284–285). Quite possibly RW, who seldom hurried himself about WW's business, had neglected to pay Wedgwood, and WW, finding that the £100 was still available, had DW write JW asking whether he thought the money should be invested in his voyage or used to pay the long-standing debt.

4–7. *Is the preface,* etc.: JW probably read WW's draft of the famous Preface before leaving Grasmere on September 29, for DW finished writing out the notes and preface the next day (*DWJ*).

4–8. *with you so soon:* Sara Hutchinson reached Grasmere on November 22 (in September DW had not expected her until spring) and stayed, except for an interval in Keswick, until late March (*DWJ; EY* 301; Letters 14, 17, 21, 24).

4–9. *Jack Hutchinsons intended marriage:* John Hutchinson, Mary's older brother, was a ham-factor at Stockton-on-Tees, Durham. His second marriage, to which JW refers, took place suddenly: "Have you heard," Mary Hutchinson wrote on October 26, "that Jack is married to Bessy Sleigh? You could not be more surprized than we were to hear of it, a few days before it happened. Sarah and Jobby [Joanna] went from S[tockton] to Penrith yesterday—Jobby was lucky to fall in for a wedding" (*MW* 1). Jack, who was in his thirty-third year when he remarried, had six children by his second wife—perhaps a "bad bargain" indeed, for he had two from his first marriage.

4–10. *the Lyoyds:* Charles Lloyd and his wife and son had moved to Brathay near Ambleside. Whatever DW had written JW about their neighborliness must have been in relief at not finding her first apprehensions about them immediately realized: "Charles Lloyd," she had told Jane Marshall on September 10, "is a man who is perpetually forming new friendships, quarrelling with his old ones, and upon the whole a dangerous acquaintance" (*EY* 296). Lloyd, in fact, suffered from mental derangement in varying degrees most of his life. After living for some time with the Coleridges and joining Coleridge and Lamb in publishing a volume of poems, he contributed by his irresponsible gossip to the temporary estrangement of Lamb and Coleridge, and tried to make DW a party to the quarrel. In April 1798 he published a novel, *Edmund Oliver,* whose hero looked like Coleridge and paralleled certain of his experiences—"my love-fit, debaucheries, leaving college, & going into the army" (*STC* 404). DW's early doubts proved to be justified: relations between the Lloyds and the Wordsworths were uneven at best. See Letters 12, 14.

4–11. *the Simpsons:* The vicar of Wythburn, his wife, son, and daughter. "The old man is upwards of eighty yet he goes a fishing to the Tarns on the hill-tops with my Brothers, and he is as active as many men of 50" (*EY* 299, DW to Jane Marshall).

4–12. *old Molly:* Molly Fisher, the Wordsworths' servant at Grasmere. She was very fond of JW and talked of sending her fortune of seven pounds "for a venture with him" (*EY* 390).

4–13. *the Clarksons:* Catherine Clarkson and her husband Thomas, who was active in the fight against the slave trade, were close friends of WW and DW after their arrival in Grasmere. The Clarksons' estate, Eusemere, by the northern end of Ullswater, was near the Wordsworths' most direct route to Penrith.

4–14. *Staple Inn:* One of the Inns of Chancery affiliated with Gray's Inn. RW's chambers were No. 11, near the present chambers (Nos. 1 through 10), on a site since occupied by the Patent Office. Coleridge in 1803 wrote that JW lived at No. 9 Southampton Buildings (*STC* 932), but his business and correspondence were conducted in his brother's chambers.

4–15. *Miss D. B:* The mother of the baptized children, Diana Walford, had been one of the Burroughs sisters, good friends of DW during her stay in Norfolk; they lived within five miles of Forncett Rectory.

4–16. *his last poem:* "Michael," begun October 12, finished December 9.

4–17. Two lines added at foot of address, but blotted out; illegible.

5–1. *the 80£:* On January 1, 1800, RW had credited DW's account with £100 received as a legacy from her uncle Christopher Crackanthorpe. Probably DW had requested that this money be deposited in a Carlisle bank to facilitate interest payments, as she had done before with her grandmother's gift. The £80 sent to Richard for John's use would have been a draft on this deposit. JW apparently gave her a note for the amount on December 6, 1800 (DCP).

5–2. *since Stoddart left you:* John Stoddart, a journalist, became acquainted with Coleridge, WW, and JW about the time of this letter. He was the author of *Remarks on Local Scenery and Manners in Scotland* (1801; see Letter 24). From 1803 to 1807 he was King's and Admiralty Advocate at Malta and was influential in persuading Coleridge to go there. His sister Sarah was the partner of Hazlitt's ill-fated first marriage. Stoddart visited the Lake District from October 22 to November 4, 1800. The day he left, WW wore himself out climbing to Grisedale Tarn and up Seat Sandal and began to suffer from piles (*DWJ*).

6–1. Some time after October 26 (*MW* 1) Mary Hutchinson left Gallow Hill to visit her brother John at Stockton-on-Tees. Someone, probably her brother Thomas, re-directed the letter, cancelling the original address, and added a note at the end, asking Mary, among other things, to bring back with her a "martingale and neck straps" which had been left at Jack's.

6–2. *your Brother Henry:* The second of the Hutchinson brothers, born 1769. He first went to sea on a trading voyage to China, served an apprenticeship on a merchant vessel, then joined the Navy. At the time of JW's letter he had left his ship, the *Edgar,* because of his captain's brutal discipline, and had probably been out of work for several months (*SH* 3 n.).

6–3. *that W^m^ should be loosing so much time:* The delay in the appearance of the *Lyrical Ballads* does not seem to have been the fault of the printer or publisher. At first WW appears to have been anxious to have Volume I in print, possibly with the idea of selling it separately: in July, 1800, a note from him on the address sheet of a letter by Coleridge to the printers ordered the poems for the first volume to be printed at once; and about August 13 he wrote Thomas N. Longman to find out whether the volume should be sent up to London immediately, leaving the still uncompleted preface to be prefixed to the second volume (*STC* 592, 617). This plan was dropped, however, and the completion of the Preface in its final form was delayed, first by the decision to omit

Christabel, next by Coleridge's failure to provide his share of *Poems on the Naming of Places.* Both omissions meant changes in the Preface and a shortage of material for the second volume. "Michael" was not completed until December 9, and the printers did not receive the last of their corrected copy until just before Christmas.

6–4. *Longman:* Thomas N. Longman, of Longman and Rees, Paternoster Row, the firm which in 1799 had bought all the copyrights of Joseph Cottle, the Bristol printer of the *Lyrical Ballads.* When the copyrights were assessed, that of the *Lyrical Ballads* was declared valueless; Longman and Rees returned it to Cottle, who made a present of it to WW. However, the sale of the volume—the 1798 edition was exhausted by mid-1800—evidently persuaded Longman that a small investment in WW's poetry might be justified; he offered WW £80 for two volumes totaling 3,250 copies (*EY* 283). JW has some pungent comments on this arrangement in the letters that follow.

6–5. *Arch:* John and Arthur Arch, of Gracechurch Street, bought most of the copies of the *Lyrical Ballads* (but not the copyright) from Cottle for publication under their imprint (first edition, second issue). The firm was evidently one of the principal outlets for the second edition, together with Longman and Rees, the publishers.

6–6. *going to Cambridge to see Christr:* CW had been a Fellow of Trinity College, Cambridge, since 1798.

6–7. About two words cancelled, illegible.

7–1. *the houses are so large,* etc.: Until 1841, the patent theatres, Drury Lane and Covent Garden, had a monopoly of legitimate drama in the London winter season. In order to make room for the playgoing public, they were built so large that only the most exaggerated kind of acting could be seen or heard. In the remoter parts of the theatres, wrote one critic in 1840, the spectator "cannot see the countenances of the performers without the aid of a pocket telescope, he cannot hear any thing except the ranted speeches." F. P. Tomlins, *A Brief View of the English Drama,* in Allardyce Nicoll, *A History of the English Drama, 1660–1900,* IV (Cambridge, 1960), 23–24.

7–2. *Pizarro:* Richard Brinsley Sheridan's popular adaptation of Augustus von Kotzebue's *Die Spanier in Peru.*

7–3. *Tales of Wonder:* A collection of folk and literary ballads (1801) edited by Matthew Gregory ("Monk") Lewis, including pieces by Southey and Scott.

7–4. *Mrs Robinsons L. Tales:* Mary Robinson, an actress known as "Perdita" and at one time mistress of the Prince of Wales, published several volumes of verse; the last, which appeared in 1800, the year of her death, was entitled *Lyrical Tales.* For a time, WW intended changing the title of his second edition of the *Lyrical Ballads* to avoid confusion, particularly as Longman and Rees published both works (*EY* 297).

7–5. *the farmers boy:* A popular poem (1800) by Robert Bloomfield (1766–1823), farm laborer and shoemaker.

7–6. *Colridges Walestein:* Coleridge's translation of Schiller's *The Piccolomini, or the First Part of Wallenstein* and *The Death of Wallenstein* had appeared in the summer of 1800. Longman gave him £50 for the work—and regretted it, for he lost £250. "I am sure," Coleridge wrote, "that Longman never thinks of me but Wallenstein & the Ghosts of his departed Guineas dance an ugly Waltz round my Idea" (*STC* 863).

7–7. *George has got a farm:* Near Bishop Middleham, Durham. It appears from Letters 8, 14, and 16 that he did not take possession before February, 1801. He lost it in 1804, "having been unfortunate and sold up" (*EY* 486, DW to Catherine Clarkson, June 24, 1804).

7–8. Two or three words cancelled, illegible.

7–9. One or two words cancelled, illegible.

8–1. *I was sworn,* etc.: The Minutes of the Court of Directors of the East India Company for January 7, 1801, record that JW was declared fitly qualified for the station of Commander, sworn in, and warned by the Chairman against "illicit trade and breaking bulk [removing part of the cargo to sell it] homewards" (IOR).

8–2. About two words cancelled, illegible.

8–3. *the L. B. are not yet arrived in town:* The second edition of the *Lyrical Ballads* was printed in Bristol by Biggs and Co.

8–4. *comfortable neighbors:* See Letter 4. CW's account of the Lloyds may not have been entirely objective: he was engaged to Charles Lloyd's sister Priscilla and, DW wrote, was "desperately in love" (*EY* 296).

8–5. Word cancelled, illegible.

9–1. The first figure of the postmark is uncertain, but the date of the letter is established by John's promise to send Mary Hutchinson the *Lyrical Ballads* next day by the coach, and by their publication date. See Letter 10.

9–2. *I have deliver'd,* etc.: Coleridge, as part of a campaign to "push the sale" of the *Lyrical Ballads,* persuaded Longman, the publisher, to send complimentary copies to several prominent people, accompanied by letters pointing out how the subject or method of the poems tended toward the same results as the recipient's achievement. Except for the letter to Fox, which was composed by WW, the letters were dictated by Coleridge, but sent out over WW's signature. Sara Hutchinson enclosed them in a letter to JW, quite possibly because he was more likely than either Longman alone or RW to see to it that the business was completed promptly. The recipients were the actress Mrs. Jordan, who, Coleridge said, "intended to sing stanzas of the Mad Mother in Pizarro if she acted Cora again"; Mrs. Barbauld, the poet; William Wilberforce (see Letter 43); the Duchess of Devonshire; Sir Bland Burges, politician and poet; and the statesman Charles James Fox (*STC* 654, 665. For the letter to Wilberforce, see *STC* 666–667; to Fox, *EY* 312–315; to Burges, *EY* 683).

9–3. Added in pencil, above the line, after "Fox": "dated Jan 14, 1801"; this note may be by Christopher Wordsworth, Jr.

9–4. *Pinny:* Probably John Frederick Pinney, who had arranged for WW and DW to live in Racedown rent free and later assisted WW in the matter of Montagu's debt.

9–5. *the Song:* "She Dwelt Among the Untrodden Ways."

9–6. *John Myers:* JW's cousin, the son of his father's sister Anne; fellow student with WW at Cambridge. For JW's later opinion of him see Letter 35.

9–7. *some of my friends,* etc.: DW has preserved one of these comments in a condensed quotation from a lost letter of JW's: "To a Lady a friend of mine I gave the 2 vol: they were both new to her. The idiot Boy of all the poems her delight; could talk of no thing else" (*EY* 320, DW to Sara Hutchinson).

9–8. *Tobin:* Probably James Tobin, brother of dramatist John Tobin. It was James whose name was worked into Coleridge's impromptu first version of the opening lines of "We Are Seven," and who entreated WW to cancel the poem before the *Lyrical Ballads* left the press, saying, "It will make you everlastingly ridiculous."

9–9. *Bertrams travels:* William Bartram, *Travels through North and South Carolina, Georgia, East and West Florida, the Cherokee Country, the Extensive Territories of the Muscogulges, or Creek Confederacy, and the Country of the Choctaws; Containing an Account of the Soil and Natural Productions of Those Regions, Together with Observations on the Manners of the Indians* (Philadelphia, 1791). Coleridge described it in a note to Sara Hutchinson as "not a Book of Travels properly speaking; but a series of [prose] poems, chiefly descriptive, occasioned by the objects which the Traveller observed" (*STC* 613 & n.). WW had seen a copy before composing "Ruth" in Germany in early 1799.

9–10. *I hope Colridge is better:* Coleridge had been bed-ridden since mid-December with rheumatic fever and hydrocele. The Wordsworths had visited him in mid-January, leaving on the 19th (*STC* 664, 666).

9–11. *Mr Myers:* The Reverend Thomas Myers, of Barton, who had married the sister of JW's father. JW, WW, and Coleridge had dined with him on October 31, 1799. He was the father of John Myers, mentioned above.

10–1. About three words cancelled, illegible.

10–2. *about 5 days:* This statement provides the best information available for establishing the publication date of the *Lyrical Ballads.*

11–1. *by the post:* JW evidently sent his second letter of the evening in the coach with the *Lyrical Ballads,* the post having already left.

11–2. About two words cancelled, illegible.

11–3. *Mr Pitt has retired,* etc.: In the face of opposition by the Cabinet and the King to his proposals for Catholic relief, Pitt submitted his resignation on February 3, 1801; the King accepted it on February 5, but relapsed into insanity (blaming Pitt for his illness). Pitt therefore kept his position until after the King's recovery, resigning on March 14.

12–1. *Peggy's Letter,* etc.: Peggy Marsh, the wife of a blacksmith at Lyme, Dorsetshire, had been the devoted servant and good friend of DW and WW at Racedown and Alfoxden. In December 1803 DW again sent her a one-pound note, explaining to RW that Peggy "has now a large family and is very poor" (*EY* 426–427).

12–2. *the money which you have in the funds:* At WW's request, RW had invested part of WW's legacy from Raisley Calvert in 3% Consols. These were sold for £277 10*s.* and the proceeds turned over to JW on March 12, in exchange for his note for £357 10*s.*—the price of the consols plus the £80 lent him by DW in December 1800 (DCP).

12–3. *Joseph W.:* Son of JW's cousin Richard Wordsworth of Branthwaite. He was a midshipman on the *Earl of Abergavenny* on her 1799 voyage; 6th mate on her first voyage under JW's command, 1801–1802; 4th mate, 1803–1804; and 3rd mate on her fatal last voyage in 1805. It was probably JW who saw to it that he was one of the men who took the ship's dispatches ashore before she sank.

12–4. *"that was its horse, its Chariot:* Cf. Line 24 of *Poems on the Naming of Places,* IV ("A narrow girdle of rough stones and crags"), *PW* II, 116.

12–5. Two or three words torn away by seal, here and on line following.

12–6. *the* Union: the legislative union of England and Ireland was effected in May, 1800.

13–1. *Madam Langleys improvements:* Mr. Langley was Thomas Hutchinson's neighbor and landlord at Gallow Hill. The penchant for improvements by both the Langleys and the Hutchinsons led to unpleasant consequences in 1803, when Mr. Langley sent the Hutchinsons a notice to leave the farm. "What is most provoking," wrote DW to Catherine Clarkson "[is] that Mrs Langley wants this Farm into her own hands merely for a little Rural place to carry her fine Ladies to drink tea at, because they admired it, and she admired it, and before Tom Hutchinson took it nobody thought anything about it and he has made all the improvements, and in short made it the place it is" (*EY* 404, October 9, 1803).

14–1. *over the mountains:* Probably from the foot of Ullswater past Grisedale Tarn to Grasmere—the reverse of the route taken by JW when he left Grasmere for the last time in the fall of 1800.

15–1. *my Uncle W*[m] *this morning:* The Reverend William Cookson.

15–2. The name is not clear. Mary, born 1790, was Canon Cookson's oldest child.

15–3. *the 2^{d} edition:* That is, the first volume, which was considered a second edition of the 1798 *Lyrical Ballads.* This distinction was continued in 1802, when the first volume was labelled "Third Edition" and the second volume "Second Edition," but was abandoned in 1805, when both volumes were marked "Fourth Edition." See *Healey,* p. 6.

15–4. *his customers complain'd,* etc.: That is, the customers who had bought the more popular second volume. In addition to the famous Preface attached to the first volume, WW at first intended to prefix an introductory essay to the second volume, but abandoned it when nearly complete because the quotations it required would have made it too long (*EY* 309).

15–5. Word cancelled, illegible.

15–6. *Wordswordsworth:* JW's haste presumably accounts for his spelling.

16–1. *the thistles beard:* Line 18. JW apparently thought he had originated the phrase, but it occurs in *An Evening Walk,* 1793 version, line 95.

16–2. The letter has been torn almost straight down both margins; about two words are missing at both ends of each line.

16–3. *that he c^{d} look his trouble in the face:* The original version of what from 1836 was line 222.

16–4. *these two days,* etc.: Line 275 in 1836 and later editions.

16–5. *that man grossly errs,* etc.: Compare lines 62 ff. in 1836 and later editions.

16–6. *W^{m} had Joanna in mind,* etc.: JW may be right. "The Pet Lamb" is ostensibly about Barbara Lewthwaite, a little girl whose beauty JW remarked on when he first arrived at Grasmere in 1800; but Barbara, as WW explained in a Fenwick note, was not the real inspiration of the poem.

16–7. About six words torn away.

16–8. The rest of the page is missing.

16–9. One or two letters cancelled, illegible.

16–10. *Betty Foy:* The doting, anxious mother in WW's "Idiot Boy."

17–1. *Cottle:* Joseph Cottle of Bristol, friend and advisor of Wordsworth and Coleridge and patron of the latter; his firm, Biggs and Cottle, printed the first edition of the *Lyrical Ballads.*

17–2. *Mr Davy:* Humphry Davy had become prominent in 1799 for his discovery of the effects of "laughing gas," nitrous oxide; his later fame rested, among other things, on his work in electrochemistry and his invention of the miner's safety lamp. A versifier himself, he had been a friend of Coleridge since late 1799.

17–3. *the 2 Editions:* That is, of course, the two volumes of *Lyrical Ballads,* 1800 (published January, 1801).

17–4. they *will be thinking,* etc.: Letter 14 mentions that WW and DW intended to go to Keswick after their return from the Clarksons'.

17–5. *Calvert offer'd them,* etc.: William Calvert, brother of the Raisley Calvert whose legacy had given WW some degree of financial independence, was rebuilding the house at Windy Brow, near Keswick, where WW and DW had spent several weeks in the spring of 1794. In a letter to Humphry Davy (February 3, 1801), Coleridge describes the plan which WW later decided against: "A Gentleman resident here [Keswick], his name Calvert, an idle, good-hearted, and ingenious man, has a great desire to commence fellow-student with me & Wordsworth in Chemistry.—He is an intimate friend of Wordsworth's—& he has proposed to Wordsworth to take a house which he (Calvert) has nearly built, called Windy Brow, in a delicious situation, scarce half a mile from Grieta Hall, the residence of S. T. Coleridge Esq. and so for him (Calvert) to live with them, i. e. Wordsworth & his Sister.—In this case he means to build a little Laboratory &c.—Wordsworth has not quite decided, but is strongly inclined to adopt the scheme, because he and his Sister have before lived with Calvert on the same footing, and are much attached to him; because my Health is so precarious, and so much injured by Wet, and his health too is, like little potatoes, no great things, and therefore Grasmere (13 miles from Keswick) is too great a distance for us to enjoy each other's Society without inconvenience as much as it would be profitable for us both; & likewise because he feels it more & more necessary for him to have some intellectual pursuit less closely connected with deep passion, than Poetry, & is of course desirous too not to be so wholly ignorant of knowleges so exceedingly important" (*STC* 670–671).

17–6. *a beginning middle—and end:* Compare the description of the same poem in Letter 16, "complete in all its parts." It would be interesting to know where JW encountered this familiar bit of Aristotle's *Poetics;* compare the passage at the beginning of Chapter 7, ". . . A tragedy is an imitation of an action that is complete in itself, as a whole of some magnitude. . . . A whole is that which has beginning, middle, and end." *Aristotle on the Art of Poetry,* ed. & tr. by Ingram Bywater (Oxford, 1909), p. 23.

18–1. Date proved by references to receipt of DW's letter (compare Letter 17).

18–2. *all the old clothes I can muster:* WW evidently felt that JW's cast-off clothing was quite good enough for "a poet living in retirement" in Grasmere. Old clothes had been one of his economies since his Racedown days (*EY* 186, DW to RW).

18–3. About three letters cancelled, illegible.

18–4. *Fox has not answered W^m^s letter:* Coleridge to Poole, February 13, 1801: "Wordsworth has received answers from all but Mr Fox—all respectful & polite, but all written *immediately* on the receipt of the Poems, & consequently expressing no Opinion" (*STC* 676). Fox did, however, reply on

May 25, naming his favorite poems ("Goody Blake and Harry Gill," "We Are Seven," "The Mad Mother," and "The Idiot Boy") but objecting gently to "The Brothers" and "Michael" because they used blank verse for a subject which was to be treated simply.

18–5. *the Ministerial changes:* See Letter 11. Pitt had resigned in February, but his retirement was delayed by the King's insanity; Addington, whom the King had asked to take the government, found that those Ministers who agreed with Pitt on the Catholic question would not join the new Cabinet.

18–6. *L. Fitzwilliam:* William Wentworth, second Earl Fitzwilliam (1748–1833), wealthy Whig and an advocate of Catholic relief. He was a lifelong friend of Fox.

19–1. *is there not a falling off?":* These words are not in the review as printed in the *British Critic.* Otherwise JW's transcription follows the published version closely, except for changes in punctuation and one or two unimportant verbal slips. "Here endeth the chapter" is of course his own comment.

19–2. One or two words missing.

19–3. Word cancelled, illegible.

20–1. The date of writing is proved by the log of the *Abergavenny,* which shows that JW paid his regulation Sunday visit to the ship on March 8, then boarded her for good on Friday, March 13 (IOR, Log 341E).

20–2. Mary had apparently commented on JW's original objection (mentioned in Letter 16) to two "low" passages in "Michael": "That he could look his trouble in the face" and " 'Well, Isabel! this scheme / These two days has been meat and drink to me.' " The fact that both Mary and JW continued to dislike the vulgarity of the first passage because the poet was the speaker is a fair measure of contemporary standards of judgment.

21–1. *Hutton Bushel:* In the North Riding of Yorkshire.

21–2. *the Beggar:* "The Old Cumberland Beggar," called in the MS simply "The Beggar."

21–3. *the convict of Wm's*, etc.: "The poem may have been that which Lewis afterwards published with the title *The Felon* ('Oh! mark his wan and hollow cheeks, and mark his eye-balls glare!')" Louis F. Peck, *A Life of Matthew G. Lewis* (Cambridge, Mass., 1961), p. 56. As Mrs. Moorman points out, it appears from JW's remark "that by now *The Convict* was regarded as something of a joke by the family" (I, 507).

21–4. *you remember the fir trees,* etc.: According to JW's description, the trees that were felled cannot have been far from the grove of Scotch firs where he loved to walk during his visit to Grasmere in 1800—a spot known to WW and DW as "John's Grove." See *Poems on the Naming of Places,* VI ("When, to the Attractions of the Busy World"). John's Grove was on the east side of the old road to Rydal from Grasmere, a little beyond where it turns to the right at How Top Farm after passing Dove Cottage and climbing the hill, and opposite the gate which the Wordsworths knew as Sara's Gate or the Wishing Gate. JW could not have been angrier if the grove itself had been cut down, but *DWJ* records several visits to it after the date of this letter, and WW told Isabella Fenwick in the early 1840's that it was still standing. Probably, as Mrs. Moorman suggests (I, 512) the trees that were cut were on the fell above the grove.

21–5. Reading uncertain.

21–6. *the antient M— is now void of obscurity:* For Coleridge's revisions of "The Rime of the Ancyent Marinere" as it had first appeared in 1798, see *STC* 598–602; among other changes, he somewhat expanded the Argument and eliminated many archaisms.

21–7. *Loshs's of Carlisle:* James Losh of Woodside, near Carlisle, met WW by 1795 and remained his correspondent and friend for several decades. He seems to have been an outspoken man who did not always confine his comments to the privacy of his diary. In 1798 he found WW "too earnest and *emphatic* in his manner of speaking in conversation" (*Moor-*

man I, 400); in 1814, WW was "less affected than formerly" (*Moorman* II, 258); he once told WW "that it was universally reported in Cumberland that he had used his Uncle's children very ill" (*EY* 185–186); and he seems to have challenged WW in 1821 on his apparent change in political opinions (*LY* 56).

21–8. *his Child,* etc.: Derwent Coleridge, who was born September 14, 1800, became dangerously ill about two weeks later and for a time was not expected to live. On January 23, 1801, however, Coleridge said that Derwent was "a fat healthy hungry pretty creature—the abstract idea of a Baby" (*STC* 668).

22–1. *instead of a M. P—:* Lewis represented the little town of Hindon, Wiltshire, from 1796 to 1802. The remark is typical of JW's attitude toward parsons, but the author of *The Monk* probably seemed equally absurd to him in either role.

22–2. *the telescope:* See Letter 18.

22–3. *Sally Lowthian:* "Their Father's old servant at Cockermouth" (MS note by Gordon Graham Wordsworth, DCP).

22–4. *Peter Crosthwaite:* Tentatively identified by Gordon Graham Wordsworth as "the Peter Crosthwaite who published the maps of the lakes in 1783"; he described himself as " 'Admiral at Keswick Regatta, who keeps the Museum at Keswick & is Guide, Pilot, Geographer & Hydrographer to the Nobility and Gentry who make the tour of the Lakes' " (MS note, DCP). See Letter 25.

22–5. *I am sorry you have not heard from Peggy,* etc.: See Letter 12.

22–6. A few letters cancelled in each case.

22–7. I *was* most eloquent: JW's emphasis on these words (shown by underlining) indicates a quiet irony, partly at his own expense, partly at Priscilla's: DW would know how "eloquent" the abnormally shy JW had been in the presence of an attractive and talkative woman.

22–8. that something *in her countenance,* etc.: JW's undefined feeling of dislike (heightened perhaps by his own almost morbid sensitivity) and his regrets on CW's behalf turned out to be well justified. Though WW in 1806 found Priscilla "a very sweet tempered woman" (*MY* 39), she had much of the instability of her more seriously deranged brother Charles. "For these last two nights," Charles wrote in 1799, "I have held her, delirious for many hours, in my arms. . . . The poor girl is so fond of me, that at times half an hours absence on my part quite oversets her" (Frederick Beaty, *The Lloyd-Manning Letters* [Bloomington, 1957], pp. 19–20). CW eventually fell heir to these nights of delirium—"*periodical* maladies," DW called them (*MY* 637). After Priscilla's death in 1815, DW wrote, ". . . There was evidently a strong tendency in Priscilla's mind, if not to insanity, to that excess of nervous irritability which puts our feelings and actions almost as much out of our own power as if we were actually what is called insane—and who knows what this might at length have become? . . . My Brother's tenderness and patience were almost beyond belief—night after night did he sit by her bedside . . . she labouring with indescribable sensations, he comforting her and waiting for the moment when he would lie down beside her. . . . Perhaps Priscilla might have suffered less if she had had a less indulgent Husband" (*MY* 695).

22–9. *Mr Benson:* Of Dale End, on the southwest side of Grasmere Lake, the Wordsworths' landlord (*DWJ,* January 31, 1802: "We paid our rent to Benson"). Was there some difficulty about repairs to Dove Cottage?

22–10. *your poor old neighbours,* etc.: WW told the story of these (unidentified) neighbors in his letter to Fox, January 14, 1801. They were both over eighty; the husband had been bedridden many months and his wife had become lame; they had long been supported by the parish, but now it appeared that they must be removed from their home and boarded out among the parish poor. The wife "was sure that 'it would burst her heart.'" He had mentioned the fact, WW added, "to shew how deeply the spirit of independence is, even yet, rooted in some parts of the country. These people could not express themselves in this way without an almost sublime conviction of the blessings of independent domestic life. If it is true, as I believe, that this spirit is rapidly disappearing, no greater curse can befal a land" (*EY* 314).

22–11. The last word of the line and all of the next line (about ten words in all) cancelled, illegible.

22–12. *letter:* Reading uncertain.

22–13. Word cancelled, illegible.

22–14. *Mr Robinson:* John Robinson, the grandson and namesake of JW's paternal grandmother's father, was a favorite of George III and held several high posts, including Secretary of the Treasury. He was the King's agent in transmitting the sums necessary to secure the election of candidates favorable to Lord North, whom he tried in vain to dissuade from an alliance with Fox, and broke with after the failure of the Coalition. From 1774 until his death in 1802 he was M. P. for Harwich. He was actively interested in the East India Company, and his influence must have been valuable to JW in a career in which influence counted heavily. He lived at Wyke Manor, Syon Hill, Isleworth. John and Thomas Myers were his first cousins once removed; Thomas Myers married his granddaughter, Lady Mary Nevill.

24–1. *the tricks that have been played me by running away:* Since "impress money" was apparently paid when a man was recruited, to be deducted from his wages at the end of the voyage, running away after signing on was common. Log of the *Abergavenny,* May 9, 1801: "PM finding Wm Jones Seaman concealed in one of the shore Boats for the purpose of escaping secured him in Irons" (IOR, Log 341E).

24–2. *Rees:* Longman's partner in the firm which published the *Lyrical Ballads.*

24–3. *poor Hartly,* etc.: On May 6, 1801, Coleridge wrote to Southey, "Dear Hartley! we are at times alarmed by the state of his Health. . . . If I were to lose him, I am afraid, it would exceedingly deaden my affection for any other children I may have—" and added the lines that appeared in 1816 as the Conclusion to *Christabel,* Part II: "A little child, a limber Elf" (*STC* 728).

24–4. *Wm is* going on *with the recluse:* An important reference. Possibly it alludes to an attempt to extend or revise an early version of *The Recluse, Part First, Book First, Home at Grasmere,* which WW had begun in early 1800. But it appears from Letters 25, 26, 27, and 29 that before April 7, 1801, JW had been sent a version of what is now called *The Prelude,* incorporating changes made after late September 1800, and it seems probable that this is the poem meant. WW, DW, and Coleridge thought of *The Prelude* as part of *The Recluse,* though not the main part; Coleridge was apparently referring to *The Prelude* when he wrote to Thomas Poole on October 14, 1803, that "Wordsworth . . . has made a Beginning to his Recluse" (*STC* 1012). JW's statements are our only evidence that WW was working on *The Prelude* between September, 1800, and December 26, 1801, when DW's journal records, "Wm. wrote part of the poem to Coleridge."

24–5. An irregular tear has left gaps varying from one to eight words, beginning at this point.

24–6. *those that were written when I was at Grasmere:* Late January–September 29, 1800.

25–1. *the daisy's,* etc.: The only certain instance of WW's borrowing an image from JW. In the letter to Lady Beaumont (August 7, 1805) enclosing a copy of his poem "To the Daisy" ("Sweet Flower! belike one day to have," etc.), WW wrote, "The following was written in remembrance of a beautiful Letter of my Brother John, sent to us from Portsmouth. . . . Some of the expressions in the Poem are the very words he used in his Letter" (*EY* 613). The following are "the expressions" as they stand in WW's letter (the poem was later revised):

> And hopeful, hopeful was the day
> When that stout Ship at anchor lay.

Beside the shores of Wight:
The May had then made all things green;
And goodly, also, to be seen
Was that proud Ship, of Ships the Queen,
His hope and his delight.

Yet then, when call'd ashore (I know
The truth of this, he told me so)
In more than happy mood
To your abode, Sweet Daisy Flowers!
He oft would steal at leisure hours;
And lov'd you glittering in the bowers,
A starry multitude.

25–2. *the Seaman's Mother:* Apparently DW's letter described an encounter near the Wishing Gate with the old woman who the following year became the subject of WW's "The Sailor's Mother." WW related the episode many years later to Miss Fenwick, misdating the poem 1800.

25–3. *in consequence of Montague:* In 1795, WW had lent Basil Montagu part of the legacy from Raisley Calvert on which WW and DW had counted for much of their support. Montagu's payments were irregular at best; from 1798 to 1800 he seems to have paid nothing, and in February 1803 he owed £454—£300 lent on an annuity bond, £100 (half of a loan to Charles Douglass taken over by Montagu) unsecured, and £54 arrears. Since 1800 Montagu had paid about £13 a quarter, but the loan, and particularly the uncertainty of getting the principal repaid, must have caused WW much uneasiness. See *EY* 183, 383.

25–4. *the longer I keep back,* etc.: That is, the longer he could retain and accumulate capital for investment in his voyages, the more he could do for his brother and sister upon his retirement. "He encouraged me," WW wrote in 1805, "to persist in the plan of life which I had adopted;

I will work for you was his language and you shall attempt to do something for the world" (*EY* 563).

25–5. *in the country:* That is, during his stay in Grasmere.

25–6. About two words missing.

25–7. *the first part of the poem:* Probably part or all of *Prelude* I. Evidently the transcript made by Sara Hutchinson omitted the beginning of the poem.

26–1. *we shall receive our dispatches,* etc.: The ship's purser travelled with her as far as the Downs; when she left the Downs for Portsmouth, he went to London, got her dispatches from the Company, and took them overland to Portsmouth.

26–2. *any thing omitted in Michael:* Lines 192–206 of "Michael" were on a page of manuscript which was overlooked by the printer. They cause no immediately obvious interruption in the poem, but they contain the story of Luke's development between the ages of five and eighteen. WW called them "absolutely necessary to the connection of the poem" (*EY* 323).

26–3. *your poor old dog:* Perhaps this was Music, the dog commemorated by WW in two poems written in 1805, "Incident Characteristic of a Favourite Dog" and "Tribute to the Memory of the Same Dog" (*PW* IV, 77–80). "The dog Music," WW noted, "died, aged and blind, by falling into a draw-well at Gallow Hill, to the great grief of the family of the Hutchinsons" (*Grosart* III, 164).

26–4. *the Stewart at Hackness:* Hackness, a few miles from Gallow Hill, has two estates, Hackness Grange and Hackness Hall. WW, DW, and several of the Hutchinsons visited Hackness from Gallow Hill two days before WW's wedding (*DWJ*). "Stewart" apparently refers to the steward of one of the estates.

26–5. *St Helena:* Apparently the last point on the voyage with a fairly frequent mail service.

27–1. *St Michaels:* São Miguel, in the Azores. On May 17,

1801, Coleridge wrote to Thomas Poole, "Captn Wordsworth (W's Brother & worthy to be so) passed two months there, & warmly recommends a wintering there, as almost a certain Cure of my Complaints" (*STC* 732–733).

27–2. *the preface to Peter Bell:* Lines 1–190 in the published version.

27–3. *the female vagrant,* etc.: The revisions of "The Female Vagrant," which was first published in the 1798 *Lyrical Ballads,* were made some time before April 9, 1801. In a letter of that date to Miss Taylor, who had congratulated him on the "genuine simplicity" of his style, WW says that in writing the poem, several years before the rest of the *Lyrical Ballads* (it is a part of *Guilt and Sorrow,* and was possibly begun in 1791), he did not follow the rule laid down in the 1800 Preface by "endeavouring to look . . . steadily at my subject." As a result "the diction . . . is often vicious, and the descriptions are often false. . . ." (*EY* 328). He follows these strictures with a list of alterations to the poem.

27–4. Two words cancelled, illegible.

27–5. *the poem to Col*[*eridge*]: *The Prelude,* probably sent in the "two large & ful sheets" of WW's poems copied for JW by Sara Hutchinson in late March (Letter 26). This reference is a further indication that WW worked on the poem after September, 1800: JW would almost certainly have seen any earlier revisions before he left Grasmere.

27–6. *I think I am sorry for him:* Because of his infatuation with Priscilla Lloyd (see Letter 22). CW was lodging in Ambleside, courting Priscilla, in late March or early April.

27–7. *Batavia:* Jakarta. A Dutch colony through most of its history, it was governed by Britain during the Napoleonic wars but subsequently returned to Holland.

27–8. *the box of old clothes:* See Letter 18. In late November, 1801, WW was still urging RW to send the box. It finally arrived in Grasmere on February 1, 1802 (*DWJ*).

27–9. *the corrections:* On March 26, WW had received from

Longman and Rees several copies of "cancelled sheets," probably those that supplied the lines missing from "Michael" plus a new errata sheet listing twenty-seven corrections and new readings. Since JW left the London area on March 19, probably before the revisions were in print, he seems to have arranged for Longman to send them to the India House to be brought by the purser with the ship's dispatches.

28–1. Having missed the post night, JW kept this letter and the one following until shortly before May 8, the date of the London postmarks. Someone, perhaps Thomas Hutchinson, has used the upper left corner of the address panel for a scratch list of small payments, possibly to hired hands at Gallow Hill.

28–2. Word cancelled, illegible.

28–3. About four words cancelled, illegible.

28–4. Word cancelled, illegible.

28–5. Word cancelled, illegible.

29–1. May 3, 1801, was a Sunday.

29–2. About two words cancelled, illegible.

29–3. Word cancelled, illegible.

29–4. *Andersons poets: The Works of the British Poets, with Prefaces, Biographical and Critical, by Robert Anderson, M. D.* London and Edinburgh, 1795. WW, in the note on "Yarrow Visited" dictated to Miss Fenwick, described his meeting with Dr. Anderson at Traquhair in 1814: ". . . I was much pleased to meet with him and to acknowledge my obligation to his Collection, which had been my brother John's companion in more than one voyage to India, and which he gave me before his departure from Grasmere never to return. Through these volumes I became first familiar with Chaucer; and so little money had I then to spare for books, that, in all probability, but for this same work, I should have known little of Drayton, Daniel, and other distinguished poets of the Elizabethan age and their immediate successors, till a much later period of my life" (*Grosart* III, 70). In Volume I of his set of Anderson's *Poets,* now in the Dove Cottage Library, WW has written "Wm. Wordsworth from his dear Brother John." Quite possibly JW did leave this volume behind when he left Grasmere for the last time in September, 1800: DW's journal shows that WW was working on his translations of Chaucer in December, 1801, and in several instances he followed the errors in Anderson's text. In that case JW sent the other volumes to London and, as he states here, took them on his 1801 voyage. In November 1802 JW promised to send the entire set to WW, since he cared only for Spenser (Vol. 2) and could buy his works in a separate edition. An alternative explanation would be that WW was mistaken about the date of the gift and that he used Coleridge's copy of Anderson in 1801 (cf. Whalley, *Coleridge,* p. 31 n.).

29–5. Logan: The Reverend John Logan, 1748–1788, a minister of Leith. Logan's ballad "The Braes of Yarrow" was a favorite with WW, who used to recite, "in his own peculiar and musical manner," one stanza of the poem which, he said, "always brings the tears to my eyes; its melancholy is so intense and indescribable" (Robert A. Willmott, *Conversations at Cambridge* [London, 1836], p. 246).

29–6. *your letter with the beginning of Peter Bell:* DW to Mary Hutchinson, April 29: ". . . I have just finished a long sheet to John filled as full as possible with poems and letter" (*EY* 332). *Peter Bell* was sent in answer to JW's request in Letter 27.

29–7. *making the corrections in the female vagrant:* That is, writing into his copy of the *Lyrical Ballads* the corrections made by WW before April 9 and apparently sent by DW with her copies of other poems before April 22 (Letter 27).

29–8. *the long poem: The Prelude.* See Letter 27.

29–9. *to have Mary H. at Grasmere so soon:* She did not come until October 25, remaining, with some intervals elsewhere, until January 22, 1802.

30–1. Mary was evidently staying at her brother George's new farm.

31–1. JW's note is written at the end of a letter from DW to Mary Hutchinson. The letter is addressed in JW's hand.

31–2. The date of the letter is established by DW's mention of having met JW the evening of the day before; the log of the *Abergavenny* shows that he left his ship at Gravesend on the 11th (IOR, Log 341E).

31–3. *But what ever fate Befal me,* etc.: Compare "Michael," lines 415–417 (1836 and later editions).

32–1. *while you remaind at Gallow Hill:* WW, DW, and Mary Hutchinson Wordsworth left Gallow Hill on William's and Mary's wedding-day, October 4, for a sort of honeymoon *à trois.*

32–2. *the passage through the Straits of Malacca:* Presumably a deviation from the route prescribed by the Company's orders.

32–3. *smuggling Camblets to China:* "Camblets," or camlets, a cloth made of silk and wool, were an important item in the East India Company's export trade with China and were supposed to be a Company monopoly. In fact, however, of the 19,733 pieces brought to China in 1801 by the Company's ships, 7,861 were "smuggled," that is, brought as part of the private trade allowance of the ships' officers (*Morse* II, 363). This was not smuggling in the usual sense; the camlets were registered in the customs house, and duty was paid on them; but the Company was determined to stop the flooding of what should have been a monopoly market. On March 27, 1802, the Court of Directors wrote as follows to two of the East India captains: "The very serious injury the Company have sustained by this violation of their most positive orders and instructions has determined the Court to proceed in the severest manner against the Offenders. . . . Every commander & officer in whose name it shall appear any Camblets, or other woollens have been imported into China will, for the first offence, be mulcted in the Sum of £5—for every piece imported [—] to be deducted from his private trade account, or levied in any other manner that may appear most eligible; and applied to the use of Poplar Hospital." A second offender was to be dismissed from the service (IOR, Miscellanies, Vol. 42, No. 342, pp. 229–231). The Court's final decision in JW's case was reached on December 21, 1802, when he was fined £210 and ordered to pay before being allowed to sail again; his chief mate, fifth mate, purser, surgeon, and surgeon's mate were also fined, as well as officers of several other ships (IOR, Court Minutes, Vol. 111A, pp. 960, 962).

32–4. About two words cancelled, illegible.

32–5. *I might perhaps speak to him,* etc.: This indifference seems to have been a permanent trait. In June, 1837, WW wrote to his daughter: "Do not my dearest Dora be hurt at your Uncle's coldness—I called him the bad Brother, he gave me so little of his time, not more I think than twenty minutes at the very utmost when I saw him in town. It is their way, and we must make allowance, taking people as they are" (*LY* 868).

32–6. *Tom Myers will loose his election:* Thomas Myers (1764–1835), son of JW's father's sister. He was in the Indian service and, probably with the help of John Robinson's influence, became Accountant-General of Bengal (*Memoirs* II, 524). DW's plan to make a home at Racedown for his illegitimate daughter (*EY* 147) never materialized. At the time of JW's letter, Myers had apparently quarreled with his patron, perhaps over the marriage referred to in Note 32–7, and was involved in a three-way race for Harwich's two seats in Parliament, running against Robinson and a James Adams. He did not lose the election—out of the thirty-seven votes cast, he had twelve, Adams ten—but he was later unseated on Adams' petition (see Letter 34).

32–7. *his marriage:* On January 2, 1802 (MS note, Gordon Graham Wordsworth), Thomas Myers, who was then thirty-seven, had married Lady Mary Nevill, aged eighteen. She was the daughter of the Earl of Abergavenny and granddaughter of Myers' erstwhile patron John Robinson, whose wife JW refers to here.

33–1. *you have been so unwell:* On October 23, DW "came home in the toothache" and was confined upstairs until the 30th (*DWJ*).

33–2. *a* horse & a Gig: RW's accounts record that the horse was a bay. In May, 1803, after JW left on his voyage, the horse was sold for £20 (DCP, note by Gordon Graham Wordsworth). Letter 35 suggests that JW sometimes rode in the saddle instead of using the gig.

33–3. *tell Wm*, etc.: WW answered this request some time during the course of the month, in a letter to RW. He advised JW to choose an edition of Spenser that included "A View of the Present State of Ireland." However, the rest of the letter (or as much of it as survives, in the *Memoirs*) is a critique of Milton's sonnets, not a list of books for shipboard reading (*EY* 378–379).

33–4. Word cancelled, illegible.

33–5. Word cancelled, illegible.

33–6. *his Letter to Mr Fox:* Coleridge's letter, signed ΕΣΤΗΣΕ ("S. T. C."), had appeared in the issue of the *Morning Post* dated November 4th. Lamb, however, in a letter dated the 4th, say he expects it the next day (*L* I, 329). It was an attack on Fox for praising the French Revolution and the French Constitution too enthusiastically, defending the Jacobins at home against repressive measures brought on by their exaggerated show of strength, and hailing the peace of Amiens because it brought ignominy to Great Britain. Charles Lamb called the letter "a violent philippic . . . a compound of expressions of humility, gentlemen-ushering-in most arrogant charges" (*L* I, 331–332, to Thomas Manning).

33–7. *Delays and Blunders:* By Frederic Reynolds, first produced October 30, 1802.

33–8. *Cook:* George Frederick Cooke, a clever but eccentric actor, was frequently drunk when he played Richard, and his performance at best seems to have been limited. "Cooke," wrote Leigh Hunt, "a square-faced, hook-nosed, wide-mouthed, malignantly smiling man, was intelligent and peremptory, and a hard hitter: he seized and strongly kept your attention; but he was never pleasant. He was too entirely the satirist, the hypocrite, and the villain. He loved too fondly his own caustic and rascally words; so that his voice, which was otherwise harsh, was in the *habit* of melting and dying away inwardly in the secret satisfaction of its smiling malignity. As to his vaunted tragedy, it was a mere reduction of Shakespeare's poetry into indignant prose. He limited every character to its worst qualities; and had no idealism, no affections, no verse" (*Autobiography of Leigh Hunt,* ed. J. E. Morpurgo [London, 1949], p. 132).

33–9. your Acct *of* $W^{m's}$ *marriage:* That is, the account that DW commented on in her last letter. This paragraph, a curious sort of joke by Lamb, Coleridge, or (as DW believed) the *Morning Post*'s editor Daniel Stuart, ran as follows: "Monday last, W. Wordsworth, Esq. was married to Miss Hutchinson, of Wykeham, near Scarborough, and proceeded immediately, with his wife and his sister, for his charming cottage in the little Paradise Vale of Grasmere. His neighbour, Mr. Coleridge, resides in the Vale of Keswick, 13 miles from Grasmere. His house, (situated on a low hill at the foot of Skiddaw, with the Derwent Lake in front, and the romantic River Greta winding round the hill) commands, perhaps, the most various and interesting prospects of any house in the island. It is a perfect *panorama* of that wonderful vale, with its two lakes, and its complete circle, or rather ellipse, of mountains" (*Moorman* I, 574–575).

33–10. Word cancelled, partly illegible.

33–11. One or two words cancelled, illegible.

33–12. we can afford it: Because of not having to pay horse-hire.

33–13. *the infamous Col. Hope:* John Hatfield, who passed himself off in the Keswick area as Alexander Hope, M.P. for

Linlithgowshire and brother of the Earl of Hopetoun. He ran up bills with the local tradesmen and, though he had a wife and children, married Mary, the daughter of an innkeeper at Buttermere, on October 2. He was caught, and hanged at Carlisle in September, 1803. Coleridge wrote several articles about him in the *Morning Post,* and Wordsworth later described how he and Coleridge had been waited on by Mary (*Prelude* VII, lines 296–329).

33–14. JW first cancelled "char[acter]" and "that," then gave up and cancelled the whole passage, thoroughly enough to make the readings difficult and uncertain. "I mean Mary" is somewhat clearer than the rest.

33–15. *I have seen Colridge:* See Letter 34.

34–1. this *most violent illness:* Gaps in DW's journal and letters leave the nature of the illness unexplained. On December 25, 1802, she wrote to RW, "I am quite recovered from my late illness," though she was still weak (*EY* 380–381).

34–2. *Mr Graham:* Business agent of William Lowther, who had succeeded to the Lonsdale viscounty on the death of his distant cousin James Lowther on May 24, 1802, and set about paying the debts which his relative had systematically evaded.

34–3. Two or three words cancelled, illegible.

34–4. *Robinson Wordsworth:* Son of JW's uncle Richard Wordsworth of Whitehaven, and brother of Captain John Wordsworth, Sr. According to Gordon Graham Wordsworth, he was Collector of Customs at Harwich and probably owed the position to his cousin John Robinson; hence the indiscretion of his attachment to Myers' interest.

34–5. *Colridge left London unexpectedly:* He arrived there on Monday, November 8, and wrote to his wife on that day, "I shall stay in Town till Wednesday or perhaps Thursday—but shall see no body but Stuart & John Wordsworth—of this you may depend" (*STC* 880). By Saturday morning he had reached New Passage, on the Gloucestershire side of the Severn Estuary, on his way to Wales.

34–6. About three words torn away.

34–7. About two words torn away.

34–8. *D*[r]*:* "Debit," applying to all the figures in the right-hand column.

34–9. *896l. 5. 10:* JW's error; the original (DCP) correctly rounds off the amount to 6*d*. Otherwise JW's copy is accurate.

34–10. *It ends,* etc.: JW's comment, not in the original bill.

35–1. DW replied to this letter on Christmas Day, 1802.

35–2. *cannons:* Reading uncertain.

35–3. *viz the E*[t] *of Aberg*[y]*:* Reading uncertain.

35–4. *she is so naughty,* etc.: Sara Hutchinson was visiting at Grasmere; she and DW had both been ill, and as late as December 25 were still too weak to walk to Brathay. See Letter 34 and *EY* 381.

35–5. *W*[ms] *sonnet to Bonaparte:* "1801" ("I grieved for Buonaparté"), written May 21, 1802, and published in the *Morning Post* on September 6.

35–6. *written:* Reading uncertain.

36–1. Thomas Wedgwood had requested between £50 and £100 worth of Chinese or India drawings; however, Coleridge offered to write JW asking him to bring them from China instead of buying them in London, and Wedgwood apparently replied that JW should forget the matter entirely (*STC* 921–922).

36–2. *Bang:* Wedgwood evidently felt that bang (marijuana), a product of Bengal, might relieve the symptoms of his illness, which Coleridge (*STC* 928) described as "a complete *taedium vitae.*" Coleridge later got him a sample of the drug from another source (*STC* 926–927).

36–3. *country Ship:* a ship trading with India.

38–1. Someone has practiced copying parts of the address: "Miss Wordsworth / Wordsworth Westmoreland."

38–2. The postmark is unclear, but the date is proved by the log of the *Abergavenny* (IOR, Log 341F).

38–3. About two words cancelled, illegible.

38–4. *in the country:* in Asia (in this case, China).

38–5. *Mr Robinsons share of the Abergany,* etc.: John Robinson does not appear on the list of owners of the *Earl of Abergavenny* who were consulted about building "on her bottom" after the wreck, but Captain Wordsworth, Sr. is the only Wordsworth whose name does appear. He may have bought Robinson's share, or it may have been sold or given to Robinson's son-in-law, Henry Nevill, second Earl of Abergavenny, who is also listed (WP).

38–6. Word (obviously "and" or "or") blotted, illegible.

39–1. *the three thousand pounds,* etc.: The money was paid to Richard on March 1, 1803 (DCP).

39–2. Word cancelled, illegible.

39–3. *now I ask you,* etc.: The question of security for JW's investment was the source of a good deal of correspondence in the Wordsworth family, with strong feelings threatening to break through the polite surface of several of the letters. See Introduction.

39–4. *the poems which Mr Cook brought me:* Richard Cooke had visited Grasmere in February and early April (*EY* 383, 384). The poems which JW names were written during WW's active period of creativity in the spring of 1802, except perhaps "The Sparrow's Nest," which, if the Isabella Fenwick note is correct in this instance, dated from 1801.

40–1. *we fell in with Admiral Lenios and his Squadron,* etc.: For the battle with Admiral Linois, see Introduction.

40–2. *your military appointment:* Like WW, Captain Wordsworth, Sr. had evidently joined one of the volunteer regiments forming to resist an expected Napoleonic invasion.

40–3. *the great Emperor of the Gauls:* Napoleon had been declared Emperor of France on May 18, 1804.

40–4. *Mr Stewart:* Cosmas Henry Stewart, purser of the *Earl of Abergavenny.*

40–5. *Ponqua's affairs:* Ponqua was a "Hong merchant," an agent assigned to an incoming ship to handle its trading arrangements. Each ship had its own Hong merchant. Fond of high living and subject to extortionate demands from the Mandarins, these merchants often found themselves in difficulties. In May, 1803, Ponqua came to James Drummond, President of the Select Committee which represented the Company in the Canton area, and presented a plan for extricating himself from a net indebtedness of almost two million dollars. Unwilling to see his business fail, the Committee offered him a profitable deal in camlets, which he accepted; but his difficulties continued and during the 1809 season he became bankrupt. He died in prison on February 15, 1811. See *Morse* II, 403 ff.; III, 110–111, 153.

41–1. *Mr Dent:* Managing owner of the *Earl of Abergavenny* (he held a 1/8 share).

41–2. *better than a China direct voyage:* A so-called "double voyage," including a stop at one of the Indian ports as well as China, greatly increased the commander's opportunities for private trade and for passengers, whose fares were his perquisite. Such voyages often yielded eight to ten thousand pounds, sometimes much more (*Cotton* 37).

41–3. *Mr Wallace:* Thomas Wallace, a paid Assistant Commissioner of the Board of Control, which, under the terms of Pitt's India Act of 1784, superintended the activities of the India House.

41–4. *Sir Francis Baring:* Member of the Court of Directors of the East India Company; he had been its chairman in 1792.

41–5. *Lushinton:* Sir Stephen Lushington, member of the Court of Directors for some years; chairman in 1790.

41–6. *he has lost one of [his] children since we sail'd:* Anna Cookson had died of scarlet fever on January 1, 1804.

41–7. *two pipes of Madeira Wine:* Madeira was often sent on the round trip to China to improve its flavor (*Morse* II, 29).

41–8. *the river:* The Pearl or Canton River.

42–1. Near the address someone has made two rough sketches and written "Mr Twoddall / Unthank." Wordsworth's acquaintance John Tweddel, about whom he inquired of James Losh in 1798 (*EY* 213), had died in Athens in 1799. Unthank Hall is two miles southeast of Haltwhistle, Northumberland, and the name also belongs to several North Country hamlets. I have no idea what the notation may mean.

42–2. *Lord Abergãny:* Henry Nevill, second Earl of Abergavenny, son-in-law of JW's patron John Robinson. JW's ship, of which the Earl was part owner, was named for him.

42–3. After the signature someone has written "Dr Johnsons Table Talk / from Boswells Life / of Johnson."

43–1. *Mr Wilberforce:* William Wilberforce was the central figure in "the Saints" or the "Clapham sect," dedicated to moral reform and abolition of the slave trade. He had studied with JW's uncle William Cookson at Cambridge.

43–2. *Thortons:* There were several Thorntons connected with the Company. Robert Thornton was a Director, first elected in 1797. Henry Thornton was, like Wilberforce and Charles Grant, a member of the "Clapham sect."

43–3. *Twinings:* Richard, later a Director (first elected 1810) and Thomas, a leading Proprietor (stockholder).

44–1. *the same vineyard:* The "Clapham sect" (see Letter 43).

44–2. From three to five words are torn off each line of the letter.

44–3. *little girl:* Dorothy Wordsworth, born August 16, 1804.

44–4. Sara Hutchinson was helping to take care of Mary Wordsworth after the birth of Dorothy.

45–1. *white wash us:* "Whitewashing" was probably the formal examination of an officer's qualifications.

45–2. *my voyage is changed,* etc.: Apparently JW expected the four captains who had prior choices to pick Bombay voyages, leaving the Bengal voyage for him. Hamilton, however, was at first given the Bengal voyage without being consulted, and JW was assigned a Bombay voyage, until Hamilton expressed a preference for it.

45–3. *they would as soon,* etc.: The *Earl of Abergavenny*

could, like the *Elphinstone,* navigate the Hooghly as safely as a much smaller ship.

45–4. *a* whole cargo *of passengers to Bengal:* Private passengers contracted with the captain for their fare; it seems never to have been lower than £100 and must often have been much more. In addition passengers sometimes paid as much as a hundred guineas for a seat at the captain's table.

45–5. *opium:* The opium trade was forbidden by the Company and, to a varying extent, by the Chinese government, but it was common and profitable.

45–6. *I have been in Bengal:* In 1798–1799, as second mate on the *Duke of Montrose.*

45–7. *the River:* The Hooghly.

45–8. *Mr Crawshay:* One of the two Crawshays who owned shares in the *Abergavenny* (WP).

45–9. *my cousin Ann:* Anne Favell (1771–1841), daughter of Richard Wordsworth of Whitehaven.

45–10. *Mr Favell:* Reverend Charles Favell, of Brington, Huntingdonshire; husband of JW's cousin Anne.

46–1. *carried away:* broke off.

46–2. *Cathead and Anchor Stock:* The cathead is the beam to which the anchor is hoisted; the anchor stock is the crossbar near the top of the anchor.

46–3. *she has received much hurt,* etc.: On January 21, the Court of Directors of the East India Company asked the Lords of the Admiralty to order His Majesty's Yard at Portsmouth to assist in repairing the *Warren Hastings* so that she could proceed as soon as possible (IOR, Miscellanies, Vol. 44). She reached Canton before the close of the 1805 season (*Morse* III, table).

46–4. *Mr Evans & his family:* Thomas Evans, described in official lists of survivors as "Senior Merchant, Bengal Establishment," had received permission on the preceding August to return to his post after having been invalided since 1792 (IOR, Miscellanies, Vol. 44, August 18, 1804). His group consisted of his daughter Emilia; his niece, Rebecca Jackson; and perhaps Mrs. Margaret Blair, who appears on one list as "Miss Evans' companion," on another as "proceeding to settle the affairs of her late husband." After the wreck, all of the party were rescued in a small boat except Mrs. Blair, who refused to leave the ship.

46–5. *we shall see Mr Stewart very soon:* That is, the purser will come with the final dispatches so that the ship can sail.

46–6. *Compn^ys^:* That is, recruits for the East India Company's army. Returns compiled after the wreck list 108 of these recruits.

46–7. *30 or 40 Kings:* The returns list 45 King's troops. There were also 32 Chinese aboard.

47–1. *36 or 38 persons:* The returns issued after the wreck give a total of 35. See Letter 49.

47–2. *to procure provisions &c for them:* This must indeed have been a problem, if meals on the *Abergavenny* were anything like those provided on the *Sir Edward Hughes* in 1797. On that ship, a meal for sixteen persons included pea soup, roast leg of mutton, hogs' puddings, two fowls, two hams, two ducks, corned round of beef, mutton pies, pork pies, mutton chops, stewed cabbage, potatoes, plum pudding, "porter, spruce beer, port wine, sherry, gin, rum, etc." (*Cotton* 75).

47–3. *In Ships Company we have 200:* The returns list 164.

47–4. Obscured by seal; possibly "The Thorn."

47–5. *my little name sake and his sister:* WW's children John and Dorothy.

48–1. *if I was* caught, etc.: Minutes of the Committee of Shipping, East India Company, February 13, 1793: "Ordered, That . . . it is the Committees positive order that not any Men belonging to his Majestys Navy be upon any consideration whatever received aboard the Companys Ships and that . . . if a Commander should be discovered to have acted contrary thereto he will most assuredly be dismissed the Companys Service" (IOR, Marine Miscellaneous Series, Vol. 24).

48–2. *our cousin Charles Robinson:* Probably a son of Admiral Hugh Robinson, whose wife was JW's cousin.

49–1. *Oby near Norwich:* This was the living, worth £400 a year, given CW in 1804 by his patron, Bishop Manners-Sutton (see Letter 42). It enabled CW to marry Priscilla Lloyd.

49–2. At right angles to the address, someone has listed the contents of a vegetable garden.

49–3. my sister: Priscilla Wordsworth.

50–1. This letter is placed after Letter 49 because of the lateness of the hour and because JW seems more certain here that the wind will permit him to sail.

50–2. *Captn Hipseley:* Lieutenant Hippisley, of the 8th Light Dragoons. He was left behind at Portsmouth when the *Abergavenny* sailed (*CN* 5).

50–3. *Mr Routledge:* A senior merchant bound for Bengal.

50–4. *and it is not possible,* etc.: But First Mate Samuel Baggot and Third Mate Joseph Wordsworth, finding that their ship had sailed without them, joined forces with Ensign Whitlow of the 22nd Foot to hire a sloop for forty guineas and stock her with two weeks' provisions. On February 3, they succeeded in overtaking the *Abergavenny* off Portland.

51–1. *Charles Thomas Coggan:* Assistant Clerk, Committee of Shipping, East India Company. Only the formal close and the signature of the letter appear to be in JW's hand.

51–2. Endorsed near seal, in unknown hand: "1st Feb. 1805 / Lre from Captn John / Wordsworth enclosing / a List of the E^{l} of Abergan^{ys} / Ship's Company. / Read in Com Shipping / —6 D^{o}"

51–3. *Feby 1st 1805:* Though this seems to be JW's last extant letter, the Minutes of the Court of Directors indicate that he wrote another on February 3, two days before he was shipwrecked (Vol. 113A, p. 1385). Letter 51 and the lists that accompanied it have been inserted in the ledger of JW's last completed voyage, 1803–1804 (IOR, Ledger 341L).

51–4. *List of the Ships Company,* etc.: These lists, signed by JW, were apparently the source of the returns issued by the Company after the wreck. Notations have been added next to some of the names—"S[aved]," "Paid," and, in four instances, a statement that the persons were saved though not on the Mayor of Weymouth's list.

INDEX

Date D-